Low Fat Baking

STEP-BY-STEP

Low Fat Baking

Carole Handslip

Photography by Amanda Heywood

ACROPOLIS
BOOKS

First published in l996 by Lorenz Books

© 1996 Anness Publishing Limited

Lorenz Books is an imprint of
Anness Publishing Limited
Boundary Row Studios
1 Boundary Row
London SE1 8HP

ISBN 1 85967 243 4

A CIP catalogue record is available from the British Library

Publisher: Joanna Lorenz
Senior Cookery Editor: Linda Fraser
Assistant Editor: Emma Brown
Designer: Alan Marshall
Photographer: Amanda Heywood

Printed and bound in Hong Kong

For all recipes, quantities are given in both metric and imperial
measures, and, where appropriate, measures are also given in standard
cups and spoons. Follow one set, but not a mixture, because they are
not interchangeable.

CONTENTS

Introduction	6
Techniques	16
SMALL BAKES AND BUNS	22
CAKES	36
SAVOURY BUNS AND SCONES	48
BREADS	60
SPECIAL OCCASION CAKES	82
Index	96

INTRODUCTION

It is generally agreed that a high fat diet is bad for us, especially if the fats are of the saturated variety. Unless you are making meringues or angel cakes, it is rarely possible to do entirely without fat in baking. However, it is possible to cut down considerably on the amount used and equally good results can be achieved using unsaturated oils instead of saturated fats.

Polyunsaturated oils such as sunflower oil, corn oil and safflower oil are excellent for most baking purposes, but choose olive oil, which is mono-unsaturated, for recipes that require a good, strong flavour. When an oil is not suitable, a soft margarine which is high in polyunsaturates is the fat to choose. Low fat spreads are ideal for spreading but not good for baking as they contain a high proportion of water.

Although cheese is high in saturated fat, its flavour makes it invaluable in many recipes. Choose either reduced-fat or half-fat varieties with a mature flavour, or much less of a highly flavoured cheese such as Parmesan. When using less fat you can add extra moisture to cakes and teabreads in the form of fresh or dried fruits. There is no need to use full cream milk – try skimmed milk or fruit juice instead. Buttermilk (the liquid left over from churning butter) is, surprisingly, virtually fat free and is perfect for soda bread and scones. Cream undoubtedly adds a touch of luxury to special occasion cakes, however, fromage frais, thick yogurt or curd cheese sweetened with honey make delicious, low fat fillings and toppings for even the most elaborate cakes.

So you will see that using less fat doesn't prevent you from making scrumptious cakes and bakes that look and taste every bit as good as those made traditionally with butter and cream. The recipes in this book are sure to inspire, impress and amaze everyone who believed low fat baking to be an idea too good to be true.

Store Cupboard

Many of the most useful and important baking ingredients are found in the store cupboard. The following guide highlights a few of the most essential items.

cracked wheat   olives   flour

bottled apricots

FLOURS

Mass-produced, highly refined flours are fine for most baking purposes, but for the very best results choose organic stone-ground flours because they will add flavour as well as texture to your baking.

Strong flour
Made from hard wheat which contains a high proportion of gluten, this flour is the one to use for bread-making.

Soft flour
This flour, sometimes called sponge flour, contains less gluten than plain flour and is ideal for light cakes and biscuits.

Wholemeal flour
Because this flour contains the complete wheat kernel, it gives a coarser texture and a good wholesome flavour to bread.

Rye flour
This dark-coloured flour has a low gluten content and gives a dense loaf with a good flavour. It is best mixed with strong wheat flour to give a lighter loaf.

NUTS

Most nuts are low in saturated fats and high in polyunsaturated fats. Use them sparingly as their total fat content is high.

HERBS AND SPICES

Chopped fresh herbs add a great deal of interest to baking. They add flavour to breads, scones and soda breads. In the absence of fresh herbs, dried herbs can be used: less is needed but the flavour is generally not as good.

Spices can add either strong or subtle flavours depending on the amount and variety used. Ground cinnamon, nutmeg and mixed spice are most useful for baking, but more exotic spices, such as saffron or cardomom, can also be used to great effect.

SWEETENERS

Unrefined sugars
Most baking recipes call for sugar; choose unrefined sugar, rather than refined sugars, as they have more flavour and contain some minerals.

Honey
Good honey has a strong flavour so you can use rather less of it than the equivalent amount of sugar. It also contains traces of minerals and vitamins.

Malt extract
This is a sugary by-product of barley. It has a strong flavour and is good to use in bread, cakes and teabreads as it adds a moistness of its own.

Molasses
This is the residue left after the first stage of refining sugar cane. It has a strong, smoky and slightly bitter taste which gives a good flavour to bakes and cakes. Black treacle can often be used as a substitute for molasses.

Fruit juice
Concentrated fruit juices are very useful for baking. They have no added sweeteners or preservatives and can be diluted as required. Use them in their concentrated form for baking or for sweetening fillings.

Pear and apple spread
This is a very concentrated fruit juice with no added sugar. It has a sweet-sour taste and can be used as a spread or blended with a little fruit juice and added to baking recipes as a sweetener.

Dried fruits
These are a traditional addition to cakes and teabreads and there is a very wide range available, including more unusual varieties such as peach, pineapple, banana, mango and pawpaw. The natural sugars add sweetness to baked goods and keep them moist, making it possible to use less fat.

dried pineapple   dried yeast

eggs

light muscovado sugar

currants　　*poppy seeds*　　*honey*　　*herbs*

fresh fruit　　*oatmeal*　　*cinnamon sticks*　　*dried apricots*　　*sesame seeds*

chestnuts

physalis

linseed

raisins　　*glacé cherries*　　*sunflower seeds*　　*olive oil*　　*pear and apple spread*　　*apricot compôte*　　*dates*

garlic

extra virgin olive oil

fresh fruit

ried onions

rolled oats　　*orange juice*

semolina

Oils, Fats and Dairy Produce

OILS AND FATS

Low fat spreads are ideal for spreading on breads and teabreads, but are unfortunately not suitable for baking because they have a high water content.

When you are baking, try to avoid saturated fats such as butter and hard margarine and use oils high in polyunsaturates such as sunflower, corn or safflower oil. When margarine is essential, choose a variety which is high in polyunsaturates.

Reduced-fat butter

This contains about 40% fat; the rest is water and milk solids emulsified together. It is not suitable for baking.

Low fat spread, rich buttermilk blend

Made with a high proportion of buttermilk, which is naturally low in fat. Unsuitable for baking.

Sunflower light

Not suitable for baking as it contains only 40% fat, plus emulsified water and milk solids.

Olive oil reduced-fat spread

Based on olive oil, this spread has a better flavour than some other low fat spreads, but is not suitable for baking.

Very low fat spread

Contains only 20–30% fat and so is not suitable for baking.

Olive oil

Use this mono-unsaturated oil when a recipe requires a good strong flavour. It is best to use extra virgin olive oil.

Sunflower oil

High in polyunsaturates, this is the oil used most frequently in this book as it has a pleasant but not too dominant flavour.

LOW FAT CHEESES

There are a lot of low fat cheeses that can be used in baking. Generally, harder cheeses have a higher fat content than soft cheeses. Choose mature cheese whenever possible as you need less of it to give a good flavour.

Cottage cheese

A low fat soft cheese which is also available in a half-fat form.

Quark

Made from fermented skimmed milk, this soft, white cheese is virtually free of fat.

Curd cheese

This is a low fat soft cheese made with either skimmed or semi-skimmed milk and can be used instead of cream cheese.

Feta cheese

This is a medium fat cheese with a firm, crumbly texture. It has a slightly sour, salty flavour which can range from bland to strong.

olive oil
sunflower oil
buttermilk blend
sunflower light
very low fat spread
olive oil reduced-fat spread
reduced-fat butter

cottage cheese
curd cheese
Mozzarella
Edam
Maasdam
feta
Cheddar
Red Leicester
soft cheese
quark

Mozzarella light
This is a medium-fat version of an Italian soft cheese.

Edam and Maasdam
Two medium fat hard cheeses well suited to baking.

Half-fat Cheddar and Red Leicester
These contain about 14% fat.

CREAM ALTERNATIVES
Yogurt and fromage frais make excellent alternatives to cream, and when combined with honey, liqueurs or other flavourings they make delicious fillings or toppings for cakes and bakes.

Fromage frais
This is a fresh soft cheese available in two grades: virtually fat free (0.4% fat), and a more creamy variety (7.9% fat).

Crème fraîche
This thick soured cream has a mild, lemony taste. Look out for half-fat crème fraîche which has a fat content of 15%.

Yogurt
Natural and flavoured yogurts can be used in place of cream. Low fat yogurt has a fat content of about 1%.

Bio yogurt
This contains bacterial cultures that aid digestion. Bio yogurt has a mild, sweet taste.

Greek yogurt
This thick, creamy yogurt is made from whole milk with a fat content of 10%. A low fat version is also available.

semi-skimmed milk

buttermilk

low fat yogurt

half-fat crème fraîche

bio yogurt

light fromage frais

eggs

LOW FAT MILKS

Skimmed milk
This milk has had virtually all fat removed leaving 0.1–0.3%. It is ideal for those wishing to cut down their fat intake.

Semi-skimmed milk
With a fat content of only 1.5–1.8%, this milk tastes less rich than full-cream milk. It is favoured by many people for everyday use for precisely this reason.

Powdered skimmed milk
A useful, low fat standby.

Buttermilk
Made from skimmed milk with a bacterial culture added, it is very low in fat.

Equipment

Baking sheet
Choose a large, heavy baking sheet that will not warp at high temperatures.

Balloon whisk
Perfect for whisking egg whites and incorporating air into other light mixtures.

Box grater
This multi-purpose grater can be used for citrus rind, fruit and vegetables, and cheese.

Brown paper
Used for wrapping around the outside of cake tins to protect the cake mixture from the full heat of the oven.

Cake tester
A simple implement which, when inserted into a cooked cake, will come out clean if the cake is ready.

Cook's knife
This has a heavy, wide blade and is ideal for chopping.

Deep round cake tin
This deep tin is ideal for baking fruit cakes.

Electric whisk
Ideal for creaming cake mixtures, whipping cream and whisking egg whites.

Honey twirl
For spooning honey without making a mess!

Juicer
Made from porcelain, glass or plastic – used for squeezing the juice from citrus fruits.

Loaf tin
Available in various sizes and used for making loaf-shaped breads and teabreads.

Measuring jug
Essential for measuring any kind of liquid accurately.

Measuring spoons
Standard measuring spoons are essential for measuring small quantities of ingredients.

Metal spoons
Large metal spoons are perfect for folding as they minimize the amount of air that escapes.

Mixing bowls
A set of different sized bowls is essential in any kitchen for whisking, mixing and so on.

Muffin tin
Shaped into individual cups, this tin is much simpler to use than individual paper cases. It can also be used for baking small pies and tarts.

Non-stick baking paper
For lining tins and baking sheets to ensure cakes, meringues and biscuits do not stick.

Nutmeg grater
This miniature grater is used for grating whole nutmegs.

Nylon sieve
Suitable for most baking purposes, and particularly for sieving foods which react adversely with metal.

Palette knife
This implement is needed for loosening pies, tarts and breads from baking sheets and for smoothing icing over cakes.

Pastry brush
Useful for brushing excess flour from pastry and brushing glazes over pastries, breads and tarts.

Pastry cutters
A variety of shapes and sizes of cutter are useful when stamping out pastry, biscuits and scones.

Rectangular cake tin
For making tray bakes and cakes, served cut into slices.

Ring mould
Perfect for making angel cakes and other ring-shaped cakes.

Sandwich cake tin
Ideal for sponge cakes; make sure you have two of them!

Scissors
Vital for cutting paper and snipping doughs and pastry.

Square cake tin
Used for making square cakes or cakes served cut into squares.

Swiss roll tin
This shallow tin is designed especially for Swiss rolls.

Vegetable knife
A useful knife for preparing the fruit and vegetables which you may add to your bakes.

Wire rack
Ideal for cooling cakes and bakes, allowing circulation of air to prevent sogginess.

Wire sieve
A large wire sieve is ideal for most baking purposes.

Wooden spoon
Essential for mixing ingredients and creaming mixtures.

rectangular cake tin

square cake tin

loaf tin

baking sheet

balloon whisk

large metal spoon *wooden spoon*

electric whisk

mixing bowls

non-stick baking paper

brown paper

scissors

sandwich cake tin

pastry brush

ring mould

cake tester

measuring jug

wire rack

deep round cake tin

pastry cutters

vegetable knife

honey twirl

wire rack

Swiss roll tin

juicer

wire sieve

nutmeg grater

cook's knife

palette knives

box grater

nylon sieve

measuring spoons

muffin tin

Facts about Fats

Most of us eat far more fat every day than the 10 g/¼ oz that our bodies need; on average we each consume about 115 g/4 oz fat each day.

Current nutritional advice isn't quite that strict on fat intake though, and it suggests that we should limit our daily intake to no more than 30% of total calories. In real terms, this means that for an average intake of 2,000 calories a day, 30% of energy would come from about 600 calories. Since each gram of fat provides 9 calories, your total daily intake should be no more than 67 g fat.

It's easy to cut down on obvious sources of fat such as butter, margarine, cream, whole milk and high fat cheeses, but watch out for "hidden" fats. Although we may think of cakes and biscuits as sweet foods, more calories come from their fat than from their sugar. Indeed, of the quarter of our fat intake that comes from non-meat sources, a fifth comes from dairy products and margarine and the rest from cakes, biscuits, pastries and other foods. The merits of low fat baking are enormous, as you are able not only to cut down on your fat intake in general, but you also

have control over exactly how much fat you and your family consume and the type of fat it is.

Fats can be divided into two main categories – saturated and unsaturated. We are all well aware of the dangers of saturated fats in relation to blocking arteries and causing coronary heart disease. Much of the saturated fat we eat comes from animal sources – meat and dairy products such as suet, lard and butter – which are solid at room temperature. However, there are also some saturated fats of vegetable origin, notably coconut and palm oils. In addition, a number of margarines are "hydrogenated", a process which increases the proportion of saturated fat they contain. Such margarines should be avoided.

Unsaturated fats can be divided into two main types: mono-unsaturated and polyunsaturated. Mono-unsaturated fats are found in various foods including olive oil, rapeseed oil and some nuts. These fats may actually help

lower blood cholesterol and this could explain why in Mediterranean countries, where olive oil is widely consumed, there is such a low incidence of heart disease.

The most familiar poly-unsaturated fats are of vegetable or plant origin and include sunflower oil, corn oil, soya oil, walnut oil and many soft margarines. It was believed at one time that it was beneficial to switch to polyunsaturated fats as they may also help lower cholesterol. Today, however, most experts believe that it is more important to reduce the total intake of all kinds of fat.

Above: *Animal products such as lard, suet, butter and some margarines are major sources of saturated fats.*

Left: *Some oils, such as olive and rapeseed, are thought to help lower blood cholesterol.*

Right: *Vegetable and plant oils and some margarines are high in polyunsaturated fat.*

The Fat and Calorie Contents of Food

This chart shows the weight of fat and the energy content of 115 g/4 oz of various foods.

FRUIT AND NUTS	Fat	Energy
Apples, eating	0.1 g	47 Kcals/197 kJ
Avocados	19.5 g	190 Kcals/795 kJ
Bananas	0.3 g	95 Kcals/397 kJ
Dried mixed fruit	1.6 g	227 Kcals/950 kJ
Grapefruit	0.1 g	30 Kcals/125 kJ
Oranges	0.1 g	37 Kcals/155 kJ
Peaches	0.1 g	33 Kcals/138 kJ
Almonds	55.8 g	612 Kcals/2560 kJ
Brazil nuts	68.2 g	682 Kcals/2853 kJ
Peanut butter, smooth	53.7 g	623 Kcals/2606 kJ
Pine nuts	68.6 g	688 Kcals/2878 kJ

DAIRY PRODUCE, FATS AND OILS	Fat	Energy
Cream, double	48.0 g	449 Kcals/1897 kJ
Cream, single	19.1 g	198 Kcals/828 kJ
Cream, whipping	39.3 g	373 Kcals/1560 kJ
Milk, skimmed	0.1 g	33 Kcals/130 kJ
Milk, whole	3.9 g	66 Kcals/276 kJ
Cheddar cheese	34.4 g	412 Kcals/1724 kJ
Cheddar-type, reduced-fat	15.0 g	261 Kcals/1092 kJ
Cream cheese	47.4 g	439 Kcals/1837 kJ
Brie	26.9 g	319 Kcals/1335kJ
Edam cheese	25.4 g	333 Kcals/1393 kJ
Feta cheese	20.2 g	250 Kcals/1046 kJ
Parmesan cheese	32.7 g	452 Kcals/1891 kJ
Greek yogurt	9.1 g	115 Kcals/481 kJ
Low fat yogurt, natural	0.8 g	56 Kcals/234 kJ
Butter	81.7 g	737 Kcals/308 kJ
Lard	99.0 g	891 Kcals/3730 kJ
Low fat spread	40.5 g	390 Kcals/1632 kJ
Margarine	81.6 g	739 Kcals/3092 kJ
Coconut oil	99.9 g	899 Kcals/3761 kJ
Corn oil	99.9 g	899 Kcals/3761 kJ
Olive oil	99.9 g	899 Kcals/3761 kJ
Safflower oil	99.9 g	899 Kcals/3761 kJ
Eggs (2, size 4)	10.9 g	147 Kcals/615 kJ
Egg white	Trace	36 Kcals/150 kJ
Egg yolk	30.5 g	339 Kcals/1418 kJ

OTHER FOODS	Fat	Energy
Sugar	0	94 Kcals/648 kJ
Chocolate, milk	30.3 g	529 Kcals/2213 kJ
Honey	0	88 Kcals/1205 kJ
Jam	0	61 Kcals/1092 kJ
Marmalade	0	61 Kcals/1092 kJ
Lemon curd	5.1 g	283 Kcals/1184 kJ

TECHNIQUES

Using Yeast

There are three main types of yeast currently available – dried, easy-blend and fresh. Easy-blend is added directly to the dry ingredients, whereas dried and fresh yeast must first be mixed with warm liquid and a little sugar to activate them.

USING DRIED YEAST

1 Measure dried yeast, then sprinkle it into the warm liquid in a jug or small bowl with a pinch of sugar. Stir well and set aside in a warm place for about 10–15 minutes.

COOK'S TIP
Dried yeast doesn't dissolve well in milk. You must either leave it for about 30 minutes to froth, or if you are in a hurry, dissolve it in a little water first.

2 When the yeast liquid becomes frothy, stir into the dry ingredients.

USING EASY-BLEND YEAST

1 Add easy-blend yeast to the dry ingredients directly from the packet. Do not dissolve it in liquid first.

COOK'S TIP
Easy-blend yeast is a special kind of dried yeast with a fine grain – it raises bread in as little as half the normal time. Bread made with this kind of yeast can be shaped after mixing and given only one rising.

USING FRESH YEAST

1 Place fresh yeast in a small bowl with a pinch of sugar and a little lukewarm water. Cream together until smooth, then leave for 5–10 minutes until frothy, before adding to the dry ingredients.

Shaping Rolls

Bread rolls can be made in all sorts of interesting shapes and sizes. Begin by dividing the dough into even-size portions.

1 To make cottage rolls, divide each portion of dough into two, making one piece about twice the size of the other. Shape both pieces into smooth balls. Dampen the top of the large ball and place the small ball on top. Push a lightly floured index finger through the middle of the dough.

2 To make clover leaf rolls, divide each portion of dough into three equal pieces. Shape each piece into a smooth ball, lightly dampen, and arrange in a clover leaf formation. Lightly press together.

3 To make knots, roll each dough portion into a fairly long sausage shape. Carefully knot the dough sausage, as you would a piece of string.

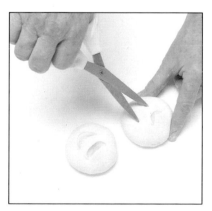

4 To make plaits, divide each dough portion into three equal pieces. Roll each piece into an even sausage shape. Dampen the three sausages at one end and pinch together. Plait the sausages loosely and pinch together at the other end, dampening lightly first.

5 To make snipped-top rolls, roll each dough portion into a smooth ball. Using a pair of kitchen scissors, make two or three snips in the top of each ball.

6 To make twists, divide each dough portion into two equal pieces. Roll each piece into an even sausage shape then twist the two pieces together, dampening at each end and pressing together firmly.

Lining Baking Tins

Ensure that your cakes and teabreads don't stick to the tin by lining the tins with greaseproof or non-stick baking paper.

LINING A ROUND TIN

1 To line a round tin, place the tin on greaseproof or non-stick baking paper and draw around the edge. Cut out two rounds that size, then cut a strip, a little longer than the tin's circumference and one and a half times its depth. Lightly grease the tin and place one paper round on the base. Make small diagonal cuts along the edge of the paper strip.

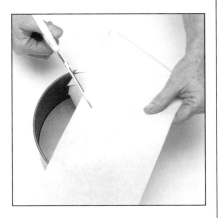

2 Put the paper strip inside the tin, with the snipped fringe along the base. Place the second paper circle in the base of the tin, covering the fringe. Grease once more.

LINING A SWISS ROLL TIN

1 To line a Swiss roll tin, cut a piece of non-stick baking paper or greaseproof paper large enough to line the base and sides of the tin. Lay the paper over the tin and make four diagonal cuts, one from each corner of the paper to the nearest corner of the tin.

2 Lightly grease the tin. Place the paper in the tin and smooth into the sides, overlapping the paper corners to fit neatly.

LINING A LOAF TIN

1 To line a loaf tin, cut a strip of greaseproof or non-stick baking paper three times as long as the depth of the tin and as wide as the length of the base.

2 Lightly grease the tin. Place the strip of paper in the tin so that the paper covers the base and comes up over both long sides.

Testing Cakes

It is very important to check that cakes and bakes are properly cooked, otherwise they can be soggy and cakes may sink in the middle.

TESTING A FRUIT CAKE

1 To test if a fruit cake is ready, push a skewer or cake tester into it: the cake is cooked if the skewer or cake tester comes out clean.

2 Fruit cakes are generally left to cool in the tin for 30 minutes. Then turn the cake out carefully, peel away the paper and place on a wire rack or board.

TESTING A SPONGE CAKE

1 To test if a sponge cake is ready, press down lightly in the centre of the cake with your fingertips – if the cake springs back, it is cooked.

2 To remove the cooked sponge cake from the tin, loosen around the edge by carefully scraping round the inside of the tin with a palette knife. Invert the cake on to a wire rack, cover with a second rack, then invert again. Remove the top rack and leave to cool.

TESTING BREAD

1 To test if a loaf of bread is ready, first loosen the edges of the loaf with a palette knife, then tip out the loaf.

2 Hold the loaf upside-down and tap it gently on the base. If it sounds hollow, the bread is cooked.

Making an Icing Bag

Being able to make your own piping bag is a very handy skill, particularly if you are dealing with small amounts of icing or several colours.

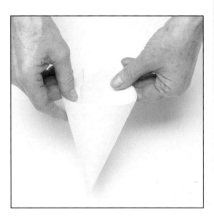

1 Fold a 25 cm/10 in square of grease-proof paper in half to form a triangle. Using the centre of the long side as the central tip, roll half the paper into a cone.

2 Holding the paper in position, continue to roll the other half of the triangle around the first, to form a complete cone.

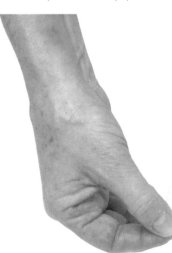

3 Holding the cone firmly, fold the end of the paper triangle over the top, into the inside of the cone to secure it. When ready to use, fill the bag no more than half full with icing, fold over the top several times to seal, then snip off the tip of the bag to the required size.

Icing a Cake

Confident icing of a cake makes all the difference to its appearance. With just a little practice, your cakes will look completely professional!

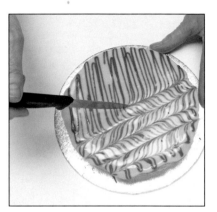

1 To create a simple zig-zag effect, ice the cake all over, then pipe lines in a different colour backwards and forwards over the top.

2 To create a feathered effect, follow step 1, then drag a knife through the icing at regular intervals in opposite directions, perpendicular to the lines.

3 To make a figure-of-eight, or a similar effect, ice the cake all over, then, using a different coloured icing, pipe figures of eight around the edge of the cake, in a steady stream.

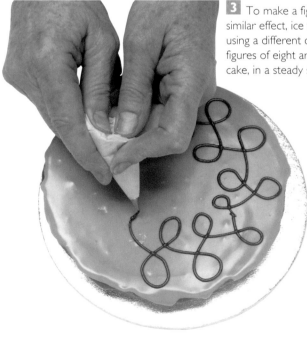

Citrus Fruits

Oranges, lemons and other citrus fruits are widely used in baking, both as flavourings and as decoration.

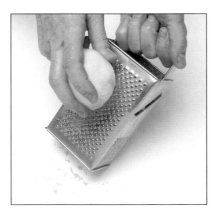

1 To grate the rind from a citrus fruit, use the finest side of a grater. Don't remove any of the white pith and brush off any rind which remains in the grater.

2 To pare the rind from a citrus fruit, use a swivel vegetable peeler. Remove the rind in strips as if peeling a potato and don't remove any of the white pith.

3 To make citrus rind shreds, or juliennes, cut strips of pared rind into very fine shreds using a sharp knife. Boil the shreds for a couple of minutes in water or sugar syrup to soften them.

Making Apricot Glaze

Apricot glaze is extremely useful for brushing over any kind of fresh fruit topping or filling to give it a lovely shiny appearance.

1 Place a few spoonfuls of apricot jam in a small pan along with a squeeze of lemon juice. Heat the jam, stirring until it is melted and runny.

2 Pour the melted jam into a wire sieve set over a bowl. Stir the jam with a wooden spoon to help it go through.

3 Return the strained jam from the bowl to the pan. Keep the glaze warm and brush it generously over the fresh fruit until evenly coated.

Banana Gingerbread Slices

Bananas make this spicy bake delightfully moist. The flavour develops on keeping, so store the gingerbread for a few days before cutting into slices, if possible.

Makes 20 slices

INGREDIENTS
275 g/10 oz/2½ cups plain flour
5 ml/1 tsp bicarbonate of soda
20 ml/4 tsp ground ginger
10 ml/2 tsp mixed spice
115 g/4 oz/⅔ cup soft light
   brown sugar
60 ml/4 tbsp sunflower oil
30 ml/2 tbsp molasses or
   black treacle
30 ml/2 tbsp malt extract
2 eggs
60 ml/4 tbsp orange juice
3 ripe bananas
115 g/4 oz/⅔ cup raisins or sultanas

1 Preheat the oven to 180°C/350°F/ Gas 4. Lightly grease and line a 28 × 18 cm/11 × 7 in shallow baking tin.

2 Sift the flour, bicarbonate of soda and spices into a mixing bowl. Place the sugar in the sieve over the bowl, add some of the flour mixture and rub through the sieve with a wooden spoon.

3 Make a well in the centre of the dry ingredients and add the oil, molasses or treacle, malt extract, eggs and orange juice. Mix thoroughly.

orange juice

plain flour

malt extract

raisins

mixed spice

soft light brown sugar

eggs

sunflower oil

bicarbonate of soda

ground ginger

bananas

molasses

5 Scrape the mixture into the prepared baking tin. Bake for about 35–40 minutes or until the centre of the gingerbread springs back when lightly pressed.

4 Mash the bananas on a plate. Add the raisins or sultanas to the gingerbread mixture then mix in the mashed bananas.

6 Leave the gingerbread in the tin to cool for 5 minutes, then turn out on to a wire rack to cool completely. Transfer to a board and cut into 20 slices to serve.

NUTRITIONAL NOTES
PER PORTION:

ENERGY 148 Kcals/621 KJ
FAT 3.07 g **SATURATED FAT** 0.53 g
CHOLESTEROL 19.30 mg **FIBRE** 0.79 g

COOK'S TIP
If your brown sugar is lumpy, mix it with a little flour and it will be easier to sift.

Lemon Sponge Fingers

These sponge fingers are perfect for serving with fruit salads or light, creamy desserts.

Makes about 20

INGREDIENTS
2 eggs
75 g/3 oz/6 tbsp caster sugar
grated rind of 1 lemon
50 g/2 oz/¹/₂ cup plain flour, sifted
caster sugar, for sprinkling

eggs

plain flour

caster sugar

lemon

VARIATION

To make Spicy Orange Fingers, substitute grated orange rind for the lemon rind and add 5 ml/1 tsp ground cinnamon with the flour.

1 Preheat the oven to 190°C/375°F/ Gas 5. Line two baking sheets with non-stick baking paper. Whisk the eggs, sugar and lemon rind together with a hand-held electric whisk until thick and mousse-like (when the whisk is lifted, a trail should remain on the surface of the mixture for at least 15 seconds). Gently fold in the flour with a large metal spoon using a figure-of-eight action.

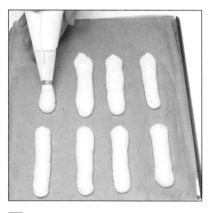

2 Place the mixture in a large piping bag fitted with a 1 cm/¹/₂ in plain nozzle. Pipe the mixture into finger lengths on the prepared baking sheets.

3 Sprinkle the fingers with caster sugar. Bake for about·6–8 minutes until golden brown, then transfer the sponge fingers to a wire rack to cool.

Snowballs

These light, almost fat-free morsels make an excellent accompaniment to yogurt ice cream.

Makes about 20

INGREDIENTS
2 egg whites
115 g/4 oz/½ cup caster sugar
15 ml/1 tbsp cornflour, sifted
5 ml/1 tsp white wine vinegar
1.5 ml/¼ tsp vanilla essence

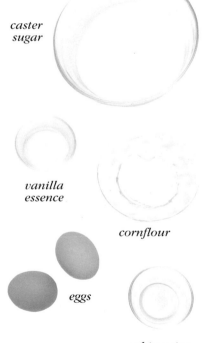

caster sugar

vanilla essence

cornflour

eggs

white wine vinegar

1 Preheat the oven to 150°C/300°F/ Gas 2 and line two baking sheets with non-stick baking paper. Whisk the egg whites in a grease-free bowl using a hand-held electric whisk until very stiff.

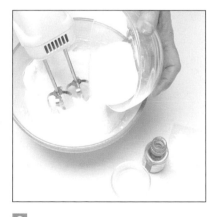

2 Add the caster sugar, a little at a time, whisking until the meringue is very stiff. Whisk in the cornflour, vinegar and vanilla essence.

VARIATION
Make Pineapple Snowballs by folding about 50 g/2 oz/¼ cup finely chopped semi-dried pineapple into the meringue.

3 Using a teaspoon, mound the mixture into balls on the prepared baking sheets. Bake for 30 minutes.

4 Cool slightly on the baking sheets, then transfer the snowballs to a wire rack to cool completely.

Filo and Apricot Purses

Filo pastry is very easy to use and is low in fat. Keep a packet in the freezer ready for rustling up a speedy tea-time treat.

Makes 12

INGREDIENTS
115 g/4 oz/³/₄ cup ready-to-eat
   dried apricots
45 ml/3 tbsp apricot compôte
   or conserve
3 amaretti biscuits, crushed
3 filo pastry sheets
20 ml/4 tsp soft margarine, melted
icing sugar, for dusting

filo pastry

*ready-to-eat
dried apricots*

*apricot
compôte*

margarine

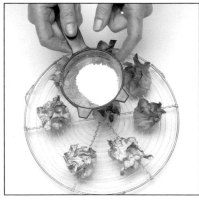
*amaretti
biscuits*

COOK'S TIP
The easiest way to crush amaretti biscuits is to put them in a plastic bag and roll with a rolling pin.

NUTRITIONAL NOTES
PER PORTION:

ENERGY 58 Kcals/245 KJ
FAT 1.85 g **SATURATED FAT** 0.40 g
CHOLESTEROL 0.12 mg **FIBRE** 0.74 g

1 Preheat the oven to 180°C/350°F/ Gas 4. Grease two baking sheets. Chop the apricots, put them in a bowl and stir in the apricot compôte. Add the crushed amaretti biscuits and mix well.

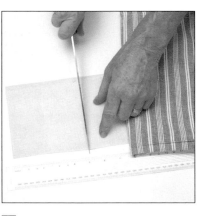

2 Cut the filo pastry into twenty-four 13 cm/5 in squares, pile the squares on top of each other and cover with a clean dish towel to prevent the pastry from drying out and becoming brittle.

3 Lay one pastry square on a flat surface, brush lightly with melted margarine and lay another square diagonally on top. Brush the top square with melted margarine. Spoon a small mound of apricot mixture in the centre of the pastry, bring up the edges and pinch together in a money-bag shape. Repeat with the remaining filo squares and filling to make 12 purses in all.

4 Arrange the purses on the prepared baking sheets and bake for 5–8 minutes until golden brown. Transfer to a wire rack and dust lightly with icing sugar. Serve warm.

Filo Scrunchies

Quick and easy to make, these pastries are ideal to serve at tea-time. Eat them warm or they will lose their crispness.

Makes 6

INGREDIENTS
5 apricots or plums
4 filo pastry sheets
20 ml/4 tsp soft margarine, melted
50 g/2 oz/¹/₃ cup demerara sugar
30 ml/2 tbsp flaked almonds
icing sugar, for dusting

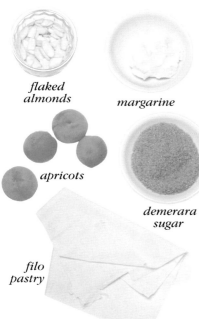

flaked almonds

margarine

apricots

demerara sugar

filo pastry

COOK'S TIP
Filo pastry dries out very quickly. Keep it covered as much as possible with a dry cloth or clear film to limit exposure to the air, or it will become too brittle to use.

NUTRITIONAL NOTES
PER PORTION:

ENERGY 132 Kcals/555 KJ
FAT 4.19 g SATURATED FAT 0.63 g
CHOLESTEROL 0 FIBRE 0.67 g

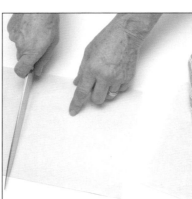

1 Preheat the oven to 190°C/375°F/ Gas 5. Halve the apricots or plums, remove the stones and slice the fruit. Cut the filo pastry into twelve 18 cm/7 in squares. Pile the squares on top of each other and cover with a clean dish towel to prevent the pastry from drying out.

2 Remove one square of filo and brush it with melted margarine. Lay a second filo square on top, then, using your fingers, mould the pastry into folds. Make five more scrunchies in the same way, working quickly so that the pastry does not dry out.

3 Arrange a few slices of fruit in the folds of each scrunchie, then sprinkle generously with the demerara sugar and flaked almonds.

4 Place the scrunchies on a baking sheet. Bake for 8–10 minutes until golden brown, then loosen the scrunchies from the baking sheet with a palette knife and transfer to a wire rack. Dust with icing sugar and serve at once.

Banana and Apricot Chelsea Buns

Old favourites are given a low fat twist with a delectable fruit filling.

Serves 9

INGREDIENTS
90 ml/6 tbsp warm skimmed milk
5 ml/1 tsp dried yeast
pinch of sugar
225 g/8 oz/2 cups strong plain flour
10 ml/2 tsp mixed spice
2.5 ml/½ tsp salt
25 g/1 oz/2 tbsp soft margarine
50 g/2 oz/¼ cup caster sugar
1 egg

FOR THE FILLING
1 large ripe banana
175 g/6 oz/1 cup ready-to-eat
   dried apricots
30 ml/2 tbsp light muscovado sugar

FOR THE GLAZE
30 ml/2 tbsp caster sugar
30 ml/2 tbsp water

dried yeast

egg

ready-to-eat dried apricots

soft margarine

muscovado sugar

mixed spice

banana

caster sugar

strong plain flour

salt

skimmed milk

COOK'S TIP

Do not leave the buns in the tin for too long or the glaze will stick to the sides, making them very difficult to remove.

1 Grease an 18 cm/7 in square cake tin. Put the warm milk in a jug. Sprinkle the yeast on top. Add a pinch of sugar to help activate the yeast, mix well and leave for 30 minutes.

2 Sift the flour, spice and salt into a mixing bowl. Rub in the margarine, then stir in the sugar. Make a central well, pour in the yeast mixture and the egg. Gradually mix in the flour to make a soft dough, adding extra milk if needed.

3 Turn the dough out on to a floured surface and knead for 5 minutes until smooth and elastic. Return to the clean bowl, cover with a damp dish towel and leave in a warm place to rise for about 2 hours until doubled in bulk.

5 Knead the risen dough on a floured surface for 2 minutes, then roll out to a 30 x 23 cm/12 x 9 in rectangle. Spread the banana and apricot filling over the dough and roll up lengthways like a Swiss roll, with the join underneath.

4 Meanwhile prepare the filling. Mash the banana in a bowl. Using kitchen scissors, snip the apricots, then stir them into the mashed banana with the sugar.

NUTRITIONAL NOTES
Per portion:

ENERGY 214 Kcals/901 KJ
FAT 3.18 g **SATURATED FAT** 0.63 g
CHOLESTEROL 21.59 mg **FIBRE** 2.18 g

6 Cut the roll into 9 pieces and place, cut side down, in the prepared tin. Cover and leave to rise in a warm place for about 30 minutes. Preheat the oven to 200°C/400°F/Gas 6.

7 Bake the buns for 20–25 minutes until golden brown and cooked in the centre. Meanwhile make the glaze. Mix the caster sugar and water in a small saucepan. Heat, stirring, until dissolved, then boil for 2 minutes. Brush the glaze over the buns while still hot, then remove the buns from the tin and leave them to cool on a wire rack.

Raspberry Muffins

These American muffins are made using baking powder and low fat buttermilk, giving them a light and spongy texture. They are delicious to eat at any time of day.

Makes 10–12

INGREDIENTS
275 g/10 oz/2½ cups plain flour
15 ml/1 tbsp baking powder
115 g/4 oz/½ cup caster sugar
1 egg
250 ml/8 fl oz/1 cup buttermilk
60 ml/4 tbsp sunflower oil
150 g/5 oz/1 cup raspberries

egg

buttermilk

sunflower oil

caster sugar

plain flour

baking powder

raspberries

NUTRITIONAL NOTES
PER PORTION:

ENERGY 171 Kcals/719 KJ
FAT 4.55 g SATURATED FAT 0.71 g
CHOLESTEROL 16.50 mg FIBRE 1.02 g

1 Preheat the oven to 200°C/400°F/ Gas 6. Arrange 12 paper cases in a deep muffin tin. Sift the flour and baking powder into a mixing bowl, stir in the sugar, then make a well in the centre.

2 Mix the egg, buttermilk and sunflower oil together in a bowl, pour into the flour mixture and mix quickly until just combined.

3 Add the raspberries and lightly fold in with a metal spoon. Spoon the mixture into the paper cases to within a third of the top.

4 Bake the muffins for 20–25 minutes until golden brown and firm in the middle. Transfer to a wire rack and serve warm or cold.

Date and Apple Muffins

You will only need one or two of these wholesome muffins per person as they are very filling.

Makes 12

INGREDIENTS
150 g/5 oz/1¼ cups self-raising wholemeal flour
150 g/5 oz/1¼ cups self-raising white flour
5 ml/1 tsp ground cinnamon
5 ml/1 tsp baking powder
25 g/1 oz/2 tbsp soft margarine
75 g/3 oz/½ cup light muscovado sugar
1 eating apple
250 ml/8 fl oz/1 cup apple juice
30 ml/2 tbsp pear and apple spread
1 egg, lightly beaten
75 g/3 oz/½ cup chopped dates
15 ml/1 tbsp chopped pecan nuts

chopped dates
egg
pecan nuts
self-raising wholemeal flour
ground cinnamon
muscovado sugar
self-raising white flour
soft margarine
apple juice
pear and apple spread
eating apple
baking powder

1 Preheat the oven to 200°C/400°F/Gas 6. Arrange 12 paper cases in a deep muffin tin. Put the wholemeal flour in a mixing bowl. Sift in the white flour with the cinnamon and baking powder. Rub in the margarine until the mixture resembles breadcrumbs, then stir in the muscovado sugar.

2 Quarter and core the apple, chop the flesh finely and set aside. Stir a little of the apple juice with the pear and apple spread until smooth. Mix in the remaining juice, then add to the rubbed-in mixture with the egg. Add the chopped apple to the bowl with the dates. Mix quickly until just combined.

3 Divide the mixture among the muffin cases.

NUTRITIONAL NOTES

PER PORTION:

ENERGY 163 Kcals/686 KJ
FAT 2.98 g **SATURATED FAT** 0.47 g
CHOLESTEROL 16.04 mg **FIBRE** 1.97 g

4 Sprinkle with the chopped pecan nuts. Bake the muffins for 20–25 minutes until golden brown and firm in the middle. Remove to a wire rack and serve while still warm.

Muscovado Meringues

These light brown meringues are extremely low in fat and are delicious served on their own or sandwiched together with a fresh fruit and soft cheese filling.

Makes about 20

INGREDIENTS
115 g/4 oz/²/₃ cup light muscovado
  sugar
2 egg whites
5 ml/1 tsp finely chopped walnuts

eggs

light muscovado sugar

walnuts

NUTRITIONAL NOTES
PER PORTION:

ENERGY 30 Kcals/124 KJ
FAT 0.34 g **SATURATED FAT** 0.04 g
CHOLESTEROL 0 **FIBRE** 0.02 g

COOK'S TIP

For a sophisticated filling, mix 115 g/4 oz/¹/₂ cup low-fat soft cheese with 15 ml/1 tbsp icing sugar. Chop 2 slices of fresh pineapple and add to the mixture. Use to sandwich the meringues together in pairs.

1 Preheat the oven to 160°C/325°F/ Gas 3. Line two baking sheets with non-stick baking paper. Press the sugar through a metal sieve into a bowl.

2 Whisk the egg whites in a grease-free bowl until very stiff and dry, then whisk in the sugar, about 15 ml/1 tbsp at a time, until the meringue is very thick and glossy.

3 Spoon small mounds of the mixture on to the prepared baking sheets.

4 Sprinkle the meringues with the chopped walnuts. Bake for 30 minutes. Cool for 5 minutes on the baking sheets, then leave to cool on a wire rack.

Apricot and Almond Fingers

These apricot and almond fingers will stay moist for several days.

Makes 18

INGREDIENTS
225 g/8 oz/2 cups self-raising flour
115 g/4 oz/²/₃ cup light muscovado
  sugar
50 g/2 oz/¹/₃ cup semolina
175 g/6 oz/1 cup ready-to-use dried
  apricots, chopped
2 eggs
30 ml/2 tbsp malt extract
30 ml/2 tbsp clear honey
60 ml/4 tbsp skimmed milk
60 ml/4 tbsp sunflower oil
few drops of almond essence
30 ml/2 tbsp flaked almonds

clear honey

sunflower oil

skimmed milk

eggs

ready-to-use dried apricots

light muscovado sugar

self-raising flour

semolina

malt extract

flaked almonds

1 Preheat the oven to 160°C/325°F/ Gas 3. Lightly grease and line a 28 × 18 cm/11 × 7 in shallow baking tin. Sift the flour into a bowl and add the muscovado sugar, semolina, dried apricots and eggs. Add the malt extract, clear honey, milk, sunflower oil and almond essence. Mix well until smooth.

2 Turn the mixture into the prepared tin, spread to the edges and sprinkle with the flaked almonds.

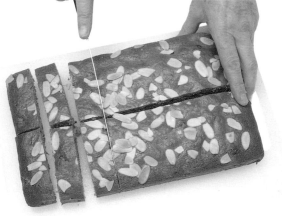

3 Bake for 30–35 minutes or until the centre of the cake springs back when lightly pressed. Transfer to a wire rack to cool. Remove the paper, place the cake on a board and cut it into 18 slices with a sharp knife.

NUTRITIONAL NOTES
PER PORTION:

ENERGY 153 Kcals/641 KJ
FAT 4.56 g **SATURATED FAT** 0.61 g
CHOLESTEROL 21.50 mg **FIBRE** 1.27 g

Coffee Sponge Drops

These are delicious on their own, but taste even better with a filling made by mixing low fat soft cheese with drained and chopped stem ginger.

Makes 12

INGREDIENTS
50 g/2 oz/¹/₂ cup plain flour
15 ml/1 tbsp instant coffee powder
2 eggs
75 g/3 oz/6 tbsp caster sugar

FOR THE FILLING
115 g/4 oz/¹/₂ cup low fat soft cheese
40 g/1¹/₂ oz/¹/₄ cup chopped
    stem ginger

instant coffee powder

eggs

plain flour

caster sugar

low fat soft cheese

stem ginger

NUTRITIONAL NOTES
PER PORTION:

ENERGY 69 Kcals/290 KJ
FAT 1.36 g SATURATED FAT 0.50 g
CHOLESTEROL 33.33 mg FIBRE 0.29 g

1 Preheat the oven to 190°C/375°F/ Gas 5. Line two baking sheets with non-stick baking paper. Make the filling by beating together the soft cheese and stem ginger. Chill until required. Sift the flour and instant coffee powder together.

2 Combine the eggs and caster sugar in a bowl. Beat with a hand-held electric whisk until thick and mousse-like (when the whisk is lifted a trail should remain on the surface of the mixture for at least 15 seconds).

3 Carefully add the sifted flour and coffee mixture and gently fold in with a metal spoon, being careful not to knock out any air.

4 Spoon the mixture into a piping bag fitted with a 1 cm/¹/₂ in plain nozzle. Pipe 4 cm/1¹/₂ in rounds on the baking sheets. Bake for 12 minutes. Cool on a wire rack. Sandwich together with the filling.

Oaty Crisps

These biscuits are very crisp and crunchy – ideal to serve with morning coffee.

Makes 18

INGREDIENTS
175 g/6 oz/1¾ cups rolled oats
75 g/3 oz/½ cup light muscovado
   sugar
1 egg
60 ml/4 tbsp sunflower oil
30 ml/2 tbsp malt extract

malt extract   *sunflower oil*

*rolled
oats*

egg

*light muscovado
sugar*

NUTRITIONAL NOTES
PER PORTION:

ENERGY 86 Kcals/360 KJ
FAT 3.59 g **SATURATED FAT** 0.57 g
CHOLESTEROL 10.70 mg **FIBRE** 0.66 g

VARIATION
To give these crisp biscuits a coarser texture, substitute jumbo oats for some or all of the rolled oats.

1 Preheat the oven to 190°C/375°F/ Gas 5. Lightly grease two baking sheets. Mix the rolled oats and brown sugar in a bowl, breaking up any lumps in the sugar. Add the egg, sunflower oil and malt extract, mix well, then leave to soak for 15 minutes.

2 Using a teaspoon, place small heaps of the mixture well apart on the prepared baking sheets. Press the heaps into 7.5 cm/3 in rounds with the back of a dampened fork.

3 Bake the biscuits for 10–15 minutes until golden brown. Leave them to cool for 1 minute, then remove with a palette knife and cool on a wire rack.

Irish Whiskey Cake

This moist rich fruit cake is drizzled with whiskey as soon as it comes out of the oven.

Serves 12

INGREDIENTS
115 g/4 oz/²/₃ cup glacé cherries
175 g/6 oz/1 cup dark muscovado
   sugar
115 g/4 oz/²/₃ cup sultanas
115 g/4 oz/²/₃ cup raisins
115 g/4 oz/¹/₂ cup currants
300 ml/¹/₂ pint/1¹/₄ cups cold tea
300 g/10 oz/2¹/₂ cups self-raising
   flour, sifted
1 egg
45 ml/3 tbsp Irish whiskey

raisins

currants

sultanas

muscovado sugar

glacé cherries

cold tea

self-raising flour

Irish whiskey

egg

COOK'S TIP
If time is short use hot tea and soak the fruit for just 2 hours.

1 Mix the cherries, sugar, dried fruit and tea in a large bowl. Leave to soak overnight until all the tea has been absorbed into the fruit.

2 Preheat the oven to 180°C/350°F/ Gas 4. Grease and line a 1 kg/2¹/₄ lb loaf tin. Add the flour, then the egg to the fruit mixture and beat thoroughly until well mixed.

NUTRITIONAL NOTES
PER PORTION:

ENERGY 265 Kcals/1115 KJ
FAT 0.88 g **SATURATED FAT** 0.25 g
CHOLESTEROL 16.00 mg **FIBRE** 1.48 g

3 Pour the mixture into the prepared tin and bake for 1¹/₂ hours or until a skewer inserted into the centre of the cake comes out clean.

4 Prick the top of the cake with a skewer and drizzle over the whiskey while the cake is still hot. Allow to stand for about 5 minutes, then remove from the tin and cool on a wire rack.

Fruit and Nut Cake

A rich fruit cake that improves with keeping.

Serves 12–14

INGREDIENTS

175 g/6 oz/1½ cups self-raising
  wholemeal flour
175 g/6 oz/1½ cups self-raising
  white flour
10 ml/2 tsp mixed spice
15 ml/1 tbsp apple and
  apricot spread
45 ml/3 tbsp clear honey
15 ml/1 tbsp molasses or black
  treacle
90 ml/6 tbsp sunflower oil
175 ml/6 fl oz/¾ cup orange juice
2 eggs, beaten
675 g/1½ lb/4 cups luxury mixed
  dried fruit
45 ml/3 tbsp split almonds
50 g/2 oz/½ cup glacé
  cherries, halved

luxury mixed dried fruit   *clear honey*   *molasses*   *mixed spice*   *eggs*

apple and apricot spread   *orange juice*   *split almonds*

self-raising white flour   *sunflower oil*

glacé cherries   *self-raising wholemeal flour*

NUTRITIONAL NOTES
PER PORTION:

ENERGY 333 Kcals/1400 KJ
FAT 8.54 g **SATURATED FAT** 1.12 g
CHOLESTEROL 29.62 mg **FIBRE** 3.08 g

1 Preheat the oven to 160°C/325°F/
Gas 3. Grease and line a deep round
20 cm/8 in cake tin. Secure a band of
brown paper around the outside.

2 Sift the flours into a mixing bowl
with the mixed spice and make a well in
the centre.

3 Put the apple and apricot spread in a
small bowl. Gradually stir in the honey
and molasses or treacle. Add to the dry
ingredients with the oil, orange juice,
eggs and mixed fruit. Mix thoroughly.

4 Turn the mixture into the prepared
tin and smooth the surface. Arrange the
almonds and cherries in a pattern over
the top. Stand the tin on newspaper and
bake for 2 hours or until a skewer
inserted into the centre comes out clean.
Transfer to a wire rack until cold, then lift
out of the tin and remove the paper.

Chocolate Banana Cake

A chocolate cake that's deliciously low fat – it is moist enough to eat without the icing if you want to cut down on calories.

NUTRITIONAL NOTES

PER PORTION:

ENERGY 411 Kcals/1727 KJ
FAT 8.79 g **SATURATED FAT** 2.06 g
CHOLESTEROL 48.27 mg **FIBRE** 2.06 g

Serves 8

INGREDIENTS
225 g/8 oz/2 cups self-raising flour
45 ml/3 tbsp fat-reduced
  cocoa powder
115 g/4 oz/²/₃ cup light muscovado
  sugar
30 ml/2 tbsp malt extract
30 ml/2 tbsp golden syrup
2 eggs
60 ml/4 tbsp skimmed milk
2 large ripe bananas
60 ml/4 tbsp sunflower oil

FOR THE ICINGS
225 g/8 oz/2 cups icing
  sugar, sifted
35 ml/7 tsp fat-reduced cocoa
  powder, sifted
15–30 ml/1–2 tbsp warm water

golden syrup

eggs

skimmed milk

icing sugar

self-raising flour

fat-reduced cocoa powder

sunflower oil

bananas

malt extract

light muscovado sugar

1 Preheat the oven to 160°C/325°F/ Gas 3. Grease and line a deep round 20 cm/8 in cake tin.

2 Sift the flour into a mixing bowl with the cocoa powder. Stir in the sugar.

3 Make a well in the centre and add the malt extract, golden syrup, eggs, milk and oil. Mash the bananas thoroughly and stir them into the mixture until thoroughly combined.

4 Pour the cake mixture into the prepared tin and bake for 1–1¼ hours or until the centre of the cake springs back when lightly pressed.

5 Remove the cake from the tin and leave on a wire rack to cool.

COOK'S TIP

This cake also makes a delicious dessert if heated in the microwave. The icing melts to a puddle of sauce. Serve a slice topped with a large dollop of fromage frais for a really special treat.

6 Reserve 50 g/2 oz icing sugar and 5 ml/1 tsp cocoa powder. Make a darker icing by beating the remaining sugar and cocoa powder with enough of the warm water to make a thick icing. Pour it over the top of the cake and spread evenly to the edges. Make a thinner, lighter icing by mixing the remaining icing sugar and cocoa powder with a few drops of water. Drizzle or pipe this icing across the top of the cake to decorate.

Mango and Amaretti Strudel

Fresh mango and crushed amaretti wrapped in wafer-thin filo pastry make a special treat that is equally delicious made with apricots or plums.

Serves 4

INGREDIENTS
1 large mango
grated rind of 1 lemon
2 amaretti biscuits
25 g/1 oz/3 tbsp demerara sugar
60 ml/4 tbsp wholemeal
  breadcrumbs
2 sheets of filo pastry, each 48 x
  28 cm/19 x 11 in
20 g/³/₄ oz/4 tsp soft margarine,
  melted
15 ml/1 tbsp chopped almonds
icing sugar, for dusting

filo pastry
mango
wholemeal breadcrumbs
lemon rind
amaretti biscuits
demerara sugar
soft margarine
chopped almonds

1 Preheat the oven to 190°C/375°F/Gas 5. Lightly grease a large baking sheet. Halve, stone and peel the mango. Cut the flesh into cubes, then place them in a bowl and sprinkle with the grated lemon rind.

2 Crush the amaretti biscuits and mix them with the demerara sugar and the wholemeal breadcrumbs.

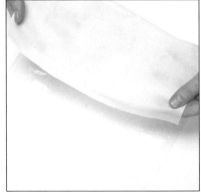

3 Lay one sheet of filo on a flat surface and brush with a quarter of the melted margarine. Top with the second sheet, brush with one-third of the remaining margarine, then fold both sheets over, if necessary, to make a rectangle measuring 28 x 24 cm/11 x 9¹/₂ in. Brush with half the remaining margarine.

4 Sprinkle the filo with the amaretti mixture, leaving a 5 cm/2 in border on each long side. Arrange the mango cubes over the top.

5 Roll up the filo from one of the long sides, Swiss roll fashion. Lift the strudel on to the baking sheet with the join underneath. Brush with the remaining melted margarine and sprinkle with the chopped almonds.

6 Bake for 20–25 minutes until golden brown, then transfer to a board. Dust with the icing sugar, slice diagonally and serve warm.

COOK'S TIP

The easiest way to prepare a mango is to cut horizontally through the fruit, keeping the knife blade close to the stone. Repeat on the other side of the stone and peel off the skin. Remove the remaining skin and flesh from around the stone.

Angel Cake

Serve this light-as-air cake with low fat fromage frais – it makes a perfect dessert.

Serves 10

INGREDIENTS
40 g/1¹/₂ oz/¹/₃ cup cornflour
40 g/1¹/₂ oz/¹/₃ cup plain flour
8 egg whites
225 g/8 oz/1 cup caster sugar, plus
 extra for sprinkling
5 ml/1 tsp vanilla essence
icing sugar, for dusting

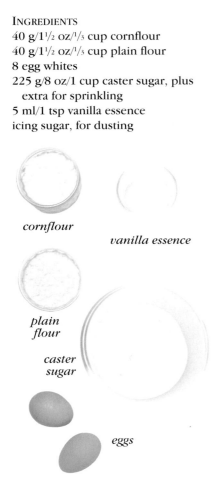

cornflour

vanilla essence

plain flour

caster sugar

eggs

NUTRITIONAL NOTES
PER PORTION:

ENERGY 139 Kcals/582 KJ
FAT 0.08 g SATURATED FAT 0.01 g
CHOLESTEROL 0 FIBRE 0.13 g

1 Preheat the oven to 180°C/350°F/ Gas 4. Sift both flours on to a sheet of greaseproof paper.

2 Whisk the egg whites in a large grease-free bowl until very stiff, then gradually add the sugar and vanilla essence, whisking until the mixture is thick and glossy.

COOK'S TIP

Make a lemony icing by mixing 175 g/6 oz/1¹/₂ cups icing sugar with 15–30 ml/1–2 tbsp lemon juice. Drizzle the icing over the cake and decorate with physalis or lemon slices and mint sprigs.

3 Gently fold in the flour mixture with a large metal spoon. Spoon into an ungreased 25 cm/10 in angel cake tin, smooth the surface and bake for about 45–50 minutes, until the cake springs back when lightly pressed.

4 Sprinkle a piece of greaseproof paper with caster sugar and set an egg cup in the centre. Invert the cake tin over the paper, balancing it carefully on the egg cup. When cold, the cake will drop out of the tin. Transfer it to a plate, decorate if liked (see Cook's Tip), then dust with icing sugar and serve.

Pear and Sultana Teabread

This is an ideal teabread to make when pears are plentiful – an excellent use for windfalls.

Serves 6–8

INGREDIENTS

25 g/1 oz/scant ¹/₃ cup rolled oats
50 g/2 oz/¹/₃ cup light muscovado
  sugar
30 ml/2 tbsp pear or apple juice
30 ml/2 tbsp sunflower oil
1 large or 2 small pears
115 g/4 oz/1 cup self-raising flour
115 g/4 oz/²/₃ cup sultanas
2.5 ml/¹/₂ tsp baking powder
10 ml/2 tsp mixed spice
1 egg

small
pears

egg

baking
powder

sunflower
oil

self-
raising
flour

rolled oats

sultanas

mixed
spice

light
muscovado
sugar

pear juice

NUTRITIONAL NOTES
PER PORTION:

ENERGY 200 Kcals/841 KJ
FAT 4.61 g **SATURATED FAT** 0.79 g
CHOLESTEROL 27.50 mg **FIBRE** 1.39 g

1 Preheat the oven to 180°C/350°F/ Gas 4. Grease and line a 450 g/1 lb loaf tin with non-stick baking paper. Put the oats in a bowl with the sugar, pour over the pear or apple juice and oil, mix well and leave to stand for 15 minutes.

2 Quarter, core and grate the pear(s). Add to the oat mixture with the flour, sultanas, baking powder, mixed spice and egg, then mix together thoroughly.

3 Spoon the mixture into the prepared loaf tin and level the top. Bake for 50–60 minutes or until a skewer inserted into the centre comes out clean.

4 Transfer the teabread on to a wire rack and peel off the lining paper. Leave to cool completely.

COOK'S TIP
Health food shops sell concentrated pear and apple juice, ready for diluting as required.

Peach Swiss Roll

A feather-light sponge enclosing peach jam –
delicious at tea time.

Serves 6–8

INGREDIENTS
3 eggs
115 g/4 oz/¹/² cup caster sugar
75 g/3 oz/³/⁴ cup plain flour, sifted
15 ml/1 tbsp boiling water
90 ml/6 tbsp peach jam
icing sugar, for dusting (optional)

plain flour

eggs

*caster
sugar*

peach jam

NUTRITIONAL NOTES
PER PORTION:

ENERGY 178 Kcals/746 KJ
FAT 2.45 g **SATURATED FAT** 0.67 g
CHOLESTEROL 82.50 mg **FIBRE** 0.33 g

COOK'S TIP
Decorate the Swiss roll with glacé
icing. Put 115 g/4 oz glacé icing in a
piping bag fitted with a small
writing nozzle and pipe lines over
the top of the Swiss roll.

1 Preheat the oven to 200°C/400°F/
Gas 6. Grease a 30 × 20 cm/12 × 8 in
Swiss roll tin and line with non-stick
baking paper. Combine the eggs and
sugar in a bowl. Beat with a hand-held
electric whisk until thick and mousse-like
(when the whisk is lifted a trail should
remain on the surface of the mixture for
at least 15 seconds).

2 Carefully fold in the flour with a
large metal spoon, then add the boiling
water in the same way.

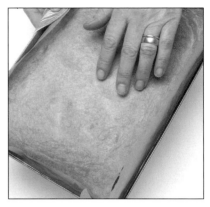

3 Spoon into the prepared tin, spread
evenly to the edges and bake for about
10–12 minutes until the cake springs
back when lightly pressed.

4 Spread a sheet of greaseproof paper
on a flat surface, sprinkle it with caster
sugar, then invert the cake on top. Peel
off the lining paper.

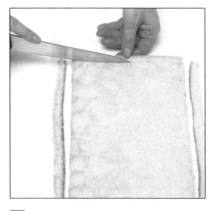

5 Neatly trim the edges of the cake.
Make a neat cut two-thirds of the way
through the cake, about 1 cm/¹/² in from
the short edge nearest you.

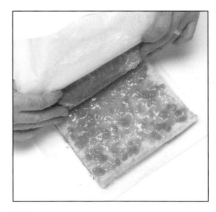

6 Spread the cake with the peach jam
and roll up quickly from the partially cut
end. Hold in position for a minute,
making sure the join is underneath. Cool
on a wire rack. Decorate with glacé icing
(see Cook's Tip) or simply dust with
icing sugar before serving.

Banana and Ginger Teabread

Serve this teabread in slices with low fat spread. The stem ginger adds an interesting flavour.

Serves 6–8

INGREDIENTS

175 g/6 oz/1½ cups self-raising flour
5 ml/1 tsp baking powder
40 g/1½ oz/3 tbsp soft margarine
50 g/2 oz/⅓ cup dark muscovado
  sugar
50 g/2 oz/⅓ cup drained stem
  ginger, chopped
60 ml/4 tbsp skimmed milk
2 ripe bananas, mashed

baking powder

stem ginger

muscovado sugar

bananas

self-raising flour

skimmed milk

soft margarine

1 Preheat the oven to 180°C/350°F/Gas 4. Grease and line a 450 g/1 lb loaf tin. Sift the flour and baking powder into a mixing bowl.

2 Rub in the margarine until the mixture resembles breadcrumbs.

VARIATION

To make Banana and Sultana Teabread, add 5 ml/1 tsp mixed spice and omit the stem ginger. Stir in 115 g/4 oz/⅔ cup sultanas.

3 Stir in the sugar. Add the ginger, milk and bananas and mix to a soft dough.

4 Spoon into the prepared tin and bake for 40–45 minutes. Run a palette knife around the edges to loosen them, turn the teabread on to a wire rack and leave to cool.

Spiced Apple Cake

Grated apple and chopped dates give this cake a natural sweetness – omit 25 g/1 oz of the sugar if the fruit is very sweet.

Serves 8

INGREDIENTS

225 g/8 oz/2 cups self-raising wholemeal flour
5 ml/1 tsp baking powder
10 ml/2 tsp ground cinnamon
175 g/6 oz/1 cup chopped dates
75 g/3 oz/¹/₂ cup light muscovado sugar
15 ml/1 tbsp pear and apple spread
120 ml/4 fl oz/¹/₂ cup apple juice
2 eggs
90 ml/6 tbsp sunflower oil
2 eating apples, cored and grated
15 ml/1 tbsp chopped walnuts

ground cinnamon

apple juice

sunflower oil

self-raising wholemeal flour

chopped walnuts

chopped dates

baking powder

muscovado sugar

pear and apple spread

eating apples

eggs

1 Preheat the oven to 180°C/350°F/Gas 4. Grease and line a deep round 20 cm/8 in cake tin. Sift the flour, baking powder and cinnamon into a mixing bowl, then mix in the dates and make a well in the centre.

2 Mix the sugar with the pear and apple spread in a small bowl. Gradually stir in the apple juice. Add to the dry ingredients with the eggs, oil and apples. Mix thoroughly.

COOK'S TIP

It is not necessary to peel the apples – the skin adds extra fibre and softens on cooking.

3 Spoon the mixture into the prepared cake tin, sprinkle with the walnuts and bake for 60–65 minutes or until a skewer inserted into the centre of the cake comes out clean. Transfer to a wire rack, remove the lining paper and leave to cool.

NUTRITIONAL NOTES

PER PORTION:

ENERGY 331 Kcals/1389 KJ
FAT 11.41 g **SATURATED FAT** 1.68 g
CHOLESTEROL 48.13 mg **FIBRE** 2.50 g

Wholemeal Herb Triangles

Stuffed with cooked chicken and salad these make a good lunchtime snack and are also an ideal accompaniment to a bowl of steaming soup.

Makes 8

INGREDIENTS

225 g/8 oz/2 cups wholemeal flour
115 g/4 oz/1 cup strong plain flour
5 ml/1 tsp salt
2.5 ml/½ tsp bicarbonate of soda
5 ml/1 tsp cream of tartar
2.5 ml/½ tsp chilli powder
50 g/2 oz/¼ cup soft margarine
60 ml/4 tbsp chopped mixed
    fresh herbs
250 ml/8 fl oz/1 cup skimmed milk
15 ml/1 tbsp sesame seeds

mixed fresh herbs

chilli powder

sesame seeds

wholemeal flour

bicarbonate of soda

cream of tartar

soft margarine

skimmed milk   *salt*   *strong plain flour*

1 Preheat the oven to 220°C/425°F/ Gas 7. Lightly flour a baking sheet. Put the wholemeal flour in a mixing bowl. Sift in the remaining dry ingredients, including the chilli powder, then rub in the soft margarine.

2 Add the herbs and milk and mix quickly to a soft dough. Turn on to a lightly floured surface. Knead only very briefly or the dough will become tough. Roll out to a 23 cm/9 in round and place on the prepared baking sheet. Brush lightly with water and sprinkle evenly with the sesame seeds.

3 Carefully cut the dough round into 8 wedges, separate them slightly and bake for 15–20 minutes. Transfer to a wire rack to cool. Serve warm or cold.

NUTRITIONAL NOTES

PER PORTION:

ENERGY 222 Kcals/932 KJ
FAT 7.22 g **SATURATED FAT** 1.25 g
CHOLESTEROL 1.06 mg **FIBRE** 3.54 g

VARIATION

To make Sun-dried Tomato Triangles, replace the fresh mixed herbs with 30 ml/2 tbsp drained chopped sun-dried tomatoes in oil, and add 15 ml/1 tbsp each mild paprika, chopped fresh parsley and chopped fresh marjoram.

Caraway Bread Sticks

Ideal to nibble with drinks, these can be made with all sorts of other seeds – try cumin seeds, poppy seeds or celery seeds.

Makes about 20

INGREDIENTS
150 ml/¹/₄ pint/²/₃ cup warm water
2.5 ml/¹/₂ tsp dried yeast
pinch of sugar
225 g/8 oz/2 cups plain flour
2.5 ml/¹/₂ tsp salt
10 ml/2 tsp caraway seeds

dried yeast

caraway seeds

plain flour

water

salt

NUTRITIONAL NOTES
PER PORTION:

ENERGY 45 Kcals/189 KJ
FAT 0.24 g **SATURATED FAT** 0.02 g
CHOLESTEROL 0 **FIBRE** 0.39 g

VARIATION

To make Coriander and Sesame Sticks, replace the caraway seeds with 15 ml/1 tbsp crushed coriander seeds. Dampen the bread sticks lightly and sprinkle them with sesame seeds before baking.

1 Grease two baking sheets. Put the warm water in a jug. Sprinkle the yeast on top. Add the sugar, mix well and leave for 10 minutes.

2 Sift the flour and salt into a mixing bowl, stir in the caraway seeds and make a well in the centre. Add the yeast mixture and gradually incorporate the flour to make a soft dough, adding a little extra water if necessary.

3 Turn on to a lightly floured surface and knead for 5 minutes until smooth. Divide the mixture into 20 pieces and roll each one into a 30 cm/12 in stick. Arrange on the baking sheets, leaving room to allow for rising, then leave for 30 minutes until well risen. Meanwhile, preheat the oven to 220°C/425°F/Gas 7.

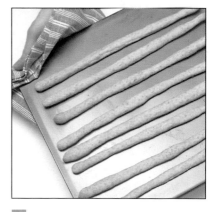

4 Bake the bread sticks for about 10–12 minutes until golden brown. Cool on the baking sheets.

Poppy Seed Rolls

Pile these soft rolls in a basket and serve them for breakfast or with dinner.

NUTRITIONAL NOTES

PER PORTION:

ENERGY 160 Kcals/674 KJ
FAT 2.42 g **SATURATED FAT** 0.46 g
CHOLESTEROL 32.58 mg **FIBRE** 1.16 g

Makes 12

INGREDIENTS
300 ml/½ pint/1¼ cups warm
  skimmed milk
5 ml/1 tsp dried yeast
pinch of sugar
450 g/1 lb/4 cups strong white flour
5 ml/1 tsp salt
1 egg, beaten

FOR THE TOPPING
1 egg, beaten
poppy seeds

strong white flour

skimmed milk

poppy seeds

egg

salt

dried yeast

1 Put half the warm milk in a small bowl. Sprinkle the yeast on top. Add the sugar, mix well and leave for 30 minutes.

2 Sift the flour and salt into a mixing bowl. Make a well in the centre and pour in the yeast mixture and the egg. Gradually incorporate the flour, adding enough of the remaining milk to mix to a soft dough.

3 Turn the dough on to a floured surface and knead for 5 minutes until smooth and elastic. Return to the clean bowl, cover with a damp dish towel and leave in a warm place to rise for about 1 hour until doubled in bulk.

4 Lightly grease two baking sheets. Turn the dough on to a floured surface. Knead for 2 minutes, then cut into 12 pieces and shape into rolls.

5 Place the rolls on the prepared baking sheets, cover loosely with a large plastic bag (ballooning it to trap the air inside) and leave in a warm place until the rolls have risen well. Preheat the oven to 220°C/425°F/Gas 7.

6 Glaze the rolls with beaten egg, sprinkle with poppy seeds and bake for 12–15 minutes until golden brown. Transfer to a wire rack to cool.

COOK'S TIP

Use easy-blend dried yeast if you prefer. Add it directly to the dry ingredients and mix with hand-hot milk. The rolls will only require one rising (see package instructions). Vary the toppings. Linseed, sesame seeds and caraway seeds are all good; try adding caraway seeds to the dough, too, for extra flavour.

Chive and Potato Scones

These little scones should be fairly thin, soft and crisp on the outside. Serve them for breakfast.

Makes 20

INGREDIENTS
450 g/1 lb potatoes
115 g/4 oz/1 cup plain flour, sifted
30 ml/2 tbsp olive oil
30 ml/2 tbsp snipped chives
salt and freshly ground black pepper
low fat spread, for topping
  (optional)

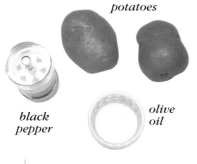

potatoes

black pepper

olive oil

chives

plain flour

salt

NUTRITIONAL NOTES
PER PORTION:

ENERGY 50 Kcals/211 KJ
FAT 1.24 g **SATURATED FAT** 0.17 g
CHOLESTEROL 0 **FIBRE** 0.54 g

1 Cook the potatoes in a saucepan of boiling salted water for 20 minutes or until tender, then drain thoroughly. Return the potatoes to the clean pan and mash them. Preheat a griddle or

2 Add the flour, olive oil and snipped chives with a little salt and pepper to the hot mashed potato in the pan. Mix to a soft dough.

COOK'S TIP
Cook the scones over a low heat so that the outsides do not burn before the insides are cooked through.

3 Roll out the dough on a well-floured surface to a thickness of 5 mm/¼ in and stamp out rounds with a 5 cm/2 in plain pastry cutter. Lightly grease the griddle or frying pan.

4 Cook the scones, in batches, on the hot griddle or frying pan for about 10 minutes, turning once, until they are golden brown on both sides. Keep the heat low. Top with a little low fat spread, if you like, and serve immediately.

Ham and Tomato Scones

These make an ideal accompaniment for soup. Choose a strongly flavoured ham and chop it fairly finely, so that a little goes a long way.

Makes 12

INGREDIENTS
225 g/8 oz/2 cups self-raising flour
5 ml/1 tsp dry mustard
5 ml/1 tsp paprika, plus extra for
   sprinkling
2.5 ml/¹/₂ tsp salt
25 g/1 oz/2 tbsp soft margarine
15 ml/1 tbsp snipped fresh basil
50 g/2 oz/¹/₃ cup drained sun-dried
   tomatoes in oil, chopped
50 g/2 oz Black Forest ham,
   chopped
90–120 ml/3–4 fl oz/¹/₂–²/₃ cup
   skimmed milk, plus extra
   for brushing

soft margarine

paprika

salt

skimmed milk

self-raising flour

fresh basil

dry mustard

sun-dried tomatoes

Black Forest ham

1 Preheat the oven to 200°C/400°F/ Gas 6. Flour a large baking sheet. Sift the flour, mustard, paprika and salt into a bowl. Rub in the margarine until the mixture resembles breadcrumbs.

2 Stir in the basil, sun-dried tomatoes and ham, and mix lightly. Pour in enough milk to mix to a soft dough.

3 Turn the dough out on to a lightly floured surface, knead lightly and roll out to a 20 × 15 cm/8 × 6 in rectangle. Cut into 5 cm/2 in squares and arrange on the baking sheet.

4 Brush lightly with milk, sprinkle with paprika and bake for 12–15 minutes. Transfer to a wire rack to cool.

NUTRITIONAL NOTES

PER PORTION:

ENERGY 113 Kcals/474 KJ
FAT 4.23 g **SATURATED FAT** 0.65 g
CHOLESTEROL 2.98 mg **FIBRE** 0.65 g

Granary Baps

These make excellent picnic fare, filled with cottage cheese, tuna, salad and low fat mayonnaise. They are also good served warm with soup.

NUTRITIONAL NOTES
PER PORTION:

ENERGY 223 Kcals/939 KJ
FAT 1.14 g **SATURATED FAT** 0.16 g
CHOLESTEROL 0 **FIBRE** 3.10 g

Makes 8

INGREDIENTS
300 ml/½ pint/1¼ cups warm water
5 ml/1 tsp dried yeast
pinch of sugar
450 g/1 lb/4 cups malted
    brown flour
5 ml/1 tsp salt
15 ml/1 tbsp malt extract
15 ml/1 tbsp rolled oats

rolled oats

brown flour

water

malt extract

salt

dried yeast

VARIATION

To make a large loaf, shape the dough into a round, flatten it slightly and bake for 30–40 minutes. Test by tapping the base of the loaf – if it sounds hollow, it is cooked.

1 Put half the warm water in a jug. Sprinkle in the yeast. Add the sugar, mix well and leave for 10 minutes.

2 Put the malted brown flour and salt in a mixing bowl and make a well in the centre. Add the yeast mixture with the malt extract and the remaining water. Gradually incorporate the flour and mix to a soft dough.

3 Turn the dough on to a floured surface and knead for 5 minutes until smooth and elastic. Return to the clean bowl, cover with a damp dish towel and leave in a warm place to rise for about 2 hours until doubled in bulk.

4 Lightly grease a large baking sheet. Turn the dough on to a floured surface, knead for 2 minutes, then divide into eight pieces. Shape into balls and flatten with the palm of your hand to make neat 10 cm/4 in rounds.

5 Place the rounds on the prepared baking sheet, cover loosely with a large plastic bag (ballooning it to trap the air inside), and leave in a warm place until the baps are well risen. Preheat the oven to 220°C/425°F/Gas 7.

6 Brush the baps with water, sprinkle with the oats and bake for about 20–25 minutes or until they sound hollow when tapped underneath. Cool on a wire rack, then serve with the low fat filling of your choice.

Curry Crackers

These spicy, crisp little biscuits are very low fat and are ideal for serving with drinks.

Makes 12

INGREDIENTS
50 g/2 oz/½ cup plain flour
1.5 ml/¼ tsp salt
5 ml/1 tsp curry powder
1.5 ml/¼ tsp chilli powder
15 ml/1 tbsp chopped fresh
  coriander
30 ml/2 tbsp water

fresh coriander

chilli powder

salt *plain flour*

water

curry powder

NUTRITIONAL NOTES
PER PORTION:

ENERGY 15 Kcals/65 KJ
FAT 0.11 g **SATURATED FAT** 0.01 g
CHOLESTEROL 0 **FIBRE** 0.21 g

1 Preheat the oven to 180°C/350°F/Gas 4. Sift the flour and salt into a mixing bowl, then add the curry powder and chilli powder. Make a well in the centre and add the chopped fresh coriander and water. Gradually incorporate the flour and mix to a firm dough.

2 Turn on to a lightly floured surface, knead until smooth, then leave to rest for 5 minutes.

VARIATIONS
Omit the curry and chilli powders and add 15 ml/1 tbsp caraway, fennel or mustard seeds.

3 Cut the dough into 12 pieces and knead into small balls. Roll each ball out very thinly to a 10 cm/4 in round.

4 Arrange the rounds on two ungreased baking sheets, then bake for 15 minutes, turning over once during cooking. Cool on a wire rack.

Oatcakes

Try serving these oatcakes with reduced-fat hard cheeses. They are also delicious topped with thick honey for breakfast.

Makes 8

INGREDIENTS
175 g/6 oz/1 cup medium oatmeal,
   plus extra for sprinkling
2.5 ml/½ tsp salt
pinch of bicarbonate of soda
15 g/½ oz/1 tbsp butter
75 ml/5 tbsp water

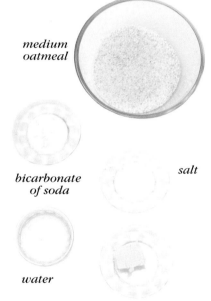

medium oatmeal

bicarbonate of soda

salt

water

butter

NUTRITIONAL NOTES
PER PORTION:

ENERGY 102 Kcals/427 KJ
FAT 3.43 g **SATURATED FAT** 0.66 g
CHOLESTEROL 0.13 mg **FIBRE** 1.49 g

COOK'S TIP
To achieve a neat round, place a 25 cm/10 in cake board or plate on top of the oatcake. Cut away any excess dough with a palette knife, then remove the board or plate.

1 Preheat the oven to 150°C/300°F/ Gas 2. Mix the oatmeal with the salt and bicarbonate of soda in a mixing bowl.

2 Melt the butter with the water in a small saucepan. Bring to the boil, then add to the oatmeal mixture and mix to a moist dough.

3 Turn the dough on to a surface sprinkled with oatmeal and knead to a smooth ball. Turn a large baking sheet upside-down, grease it, sprinkle it lightly with oatmeal and place the ball of dough on top. Sprinkle the dough with oatmeal, then roll out to a 25 cm/10 in round.

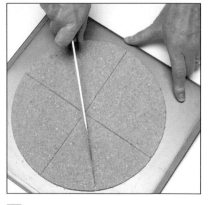

4 Cut the round into 8 sections, ease them apart slightly and bake for about 50–60 minutes until crisp. Leave to cool on the baking sheet, then remove the oatcakes with a palette knife.

Drop Scones

These little scones are delicious spread with jam.

Makes 18

INGREDIENTS
225 g/8 oz/2 cups self-raising flour
2.5 ml/¹/₂ tsp salt
15 ml/1 tbsp caster sugar
1 egg, beaten
300 ml/¹/₂ pint/1¹/₄ cups skimmed
milk

egg

*self-raising
flour*

salt

*skimmed
milk*

caster sugar

1 Preheat a griddle, heavy-based frying pan or an electric frying pan. Sift the flour and salt into a mixing bowl. Stir in the sugar and make a well in the centre.

2 Add the egg and half the milk, then gradually incorporate the surrounding flour to make a smooth batter. Beat in the remaining milk.

NUTRITIONAL NOTES
PER PORTION:

ENERGY 64 Kcals/270 KJ
FAT 1.09 g **SATURATED FAT** 0.20 g
CHOLESTEROL 11.03 mg **FIBRE** 0.43 g

VARIATION

For savoury scones, omit the sugar and add 2 chopped spring onions and 15 ml/1 tbsp freshly grated Parmesan cheese to the batter. Serve with cottage cheese.

3 Lightly grease the griddle or pan. Drop tablespoons of the batter on to the surface, leaving them until they bubble and the bubbles begin to burst.

4 Turn the drop scones over with a palette knife and cook until the underside is golden brown. Keep the cooked drop scones warm and moist by wrapping them in a clean napkin while cooking successive batches.

Pineapple and Cinnamon Drop Scones

Making the batter with pineapple juice instead of milk cuts down on fat and adds to the taste.

Makes 24

INGREDIENTS

115 g/4 oz/1 cup self-raising wholemeal flour

115 g/4 oz/1 cup self-raising white flour

5 ml/1 tsp ground cinnamon

15 ml/1 tbsp caster sugar

1 egg

300 ml/¹⁄₂ pint/1¹⁄₄ cups pineapple juice

75 g/3 oz/¹⁄₂ cup semi-dried pineapple, chopped

egg

semi-dried pineapple

pineapple juice

self-raising wholemeal flour

caster sugar

ground cinnamon

self-raising white flour

NUTRITIONAL NOTES

PER PORTION:

ENERGY 51 Kcals/215 KJ
FAT 0.81 g **SATURATED FAT** 0.14 g
CHOLESTEROL 8.02 mg **FIBRE** 0.76 g

1 Preheat a griddle, heavy-based frying pan or an electric frying pan. Put the wholemeal flour in a mixing bowl. Sift in the white flour, add the cinnamon and sugar and make a well in the centre.

2 Add the egg with half the pineapple juice and gradually incorporate the surrounding flour to make a smooth batter. Beat in the remaining juice with the chopped pineapple.

COOK'S TIP

Drop scones do not keep well and are best eaten freshly cooked.

3 Lightly grease the griddle or pan. Drop tablespoons of the batter on to the surface, leaving them until they bubble and the bubbles begin to burst.

4 Turn the drop scones with a palette knife and cook until the underside is golden brown. Keep the cooked scones warm and moist by wrapping them in a clean napkin while continuing to cook successive batches.

Soda Bread

Finding the bread bin empty need never be a problem when your repertoire includes a recipe for soda bread. It takes only a few minutes to make and needs no rising or proving. If possible eat soda bread while still warm from the oven as it does not keep well.

Serves 8

INGREDIENTS
450 g/1 lb/4 cups plain flour
5 ml/1 tsp salt
5 ml/1 tsp bicarbonate of soda
5 ml/1 tsp cream of tartar
350 ml/12 fl oz/1½ cups buttermilk

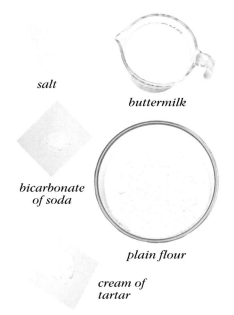

salt

buttermilk

bicarbonate of soda

plain flour

cream of tartar

1 Preheat the oven to 220°C/425°F/Gas 7. Flour a baking sheet. Sift all the dry ingredients into a mixing bowl and make a well in the centre.

NUTRITIONAL NOTES
PER PORTION:

ENERGY 230 Kcals/967 KJ
FAT 1.03 g **SATURATED FAT** 0.24 g
CHOLESTEROL 0.88 mg **FIBRE** 1.94 g

COOK'S TIP
Soda bread needs a light hand. The ingredients should be bound together quickly in the bowl and kneaded very briefly. The aim is just to get rid of the largest cracks, as the dough will become tough if it is handled for too long.

2 Add the buttermilk and mix quickly to a soft dough. Turn on to a floured surface and knead lightly. Shape into a round about 18 cm/7 in in diameter and place on the baking sheet.

3 Cut a deep cross on top of the loaf and sprinkle with a little flour. Bake for 25–30 minutes, then transfer the soda bread to a wire rack to cool.

Parma Ham and Parmesan Bread

This nourishing bread is almost a meal in itself.

Serves 8

INGREDIENTS

225 g/8 oz/2 cups self-raising
   wholemeal flour
225 g/8 oz/2 cups self-raising
   white flour
5 ml/1 tsp baking powder
5 ml/1 tsp salt
5 ml/1 tsp freshly ground
   black pepper
75 g/3 oz Parma ham, chopped
25 g/1 oz/2 tbsp freshly grated
   Parmesan cheese
30 ml/2 tbsp chopped fresh parsley
45 ml/3 tbsp Meaux mustard
350 ml/12 fl oz/1½ cups buttermilk
skimmed milk, to glaze

parsley

salt

*Parmesan
cheese*

*black
pepper*

*self-raising
wholemeal flour*

*self-raising
white flour*

*Meaux
mustard*

buttermilk

Parma ham

*baking
powder*

1 Preheat the oven to 200°C/400°F/
Gas 6. Flour a baking sheet. Place the
wholemeal flour in a bowl and sift in the
white flour, baking powder and salt. Add
the pepper and the ham. Set aside about
15 ml/1 tbsp of the grated Parmesan and
stir the rest into the flour mixture. Stir in
the parsley. Make a well in the centre.

2 Mix the mustard and buttermilk in a
jug, pour into the flour mixture and
quickly mix to a soft dough.

3 Turn the dough on to a floured
surface and knead briefly. Shape into an
oval loaf, brush with milk and sprinkle
with the remaining cheese. Place the loaf
on the prepared baking sheet.

4 Bake the loaf for 25–30 minutes, or
until golden brown. Transfer to a wire
rack to cool.

NUTRITIONAL NOTES

PER PORTION:

ENERGY 250 Kcals/1053 KJ
FAT 3.65 g **SATURATED FAT** 1.30 g
CHOLESTEROL 7.09 mg **FIBRE** 3.81 g

Austrian Three-Grain Bread

A mixture of grains gives this close-textured bread a delightful nutty flavour. Make two smaller twists if preferred.

Serves 8–10

INGREDIENTS
475 ml/16 fl oz/2 cups warm water
10 ml/2 tsp dried yeast
pinch of sugar
225 g/8 oz/2 cups strong white flour
7.5 ml/1½ tsp salt
225 g/8 oz/2 cups malted
    brown flour
225 g/8 oz/2 cups rye flour
30 ml/2 tbsp linseed
75 g/3 oz/½ cup medium oatmeal
45 ml/3 tbsp sunflower seeds
30 ml/2 tbsp malt extract

medium oatmeal
sunflower seeds
strong white flour
dried yeast
linseed
malt extract
water
rye flour
malted brown flour
salt

1 Put half the water in a jug. Sprinkle the yeast on top. Add the sugar, mix well and leave for 10 minutes.

2 Sift the white flour and salt into a mixing bowl and add the other flours. Set aside 5 ml/1 tsp of the linseed and add the rest to the flour mixture with the oatmeal and sunflower seeds. Make a well in the centre.

3 Add the yeast mixture to the bowl with the malt extract and the remaining water. Gradually incorporate the flour.

4 Mix to a soft dough, adding extra water if necessary. Turn out on to a floured surface and knead for about 5 minutes until smooth and elastic. Return to the clean bowl, cover with a damp dish towel and leave to rise for about 2 hours until doubled in bulk.

5 Flour a baking sheet. Turn the dough on to a floured surface, knead for 2 minutes then divide in half. Roll each half into a 30 cm/12 in long sausage.

6 Twist the two sausages together, dampen the ends and press to seal. Lift the twist on to the prepared baking sheet. Brush it with water, sprinkle with the remaining linseed and cover loosely with a large plastic bag (ballooning it to trap the air inside). Leave in a warm place until well risen. Preheat the oven to 220°C/425°F/Gas 7.

7 Bake the loaf for 10 minutes, then lower the oven temperature to 200°C/400°F/Gas 6 and cook for 20 minutes more, or until the loaf sounds hollow when it is tapped underneath. Transfer to a wire rack to cool.

NUTRITIONAL NOTES
PER PORTION:

ENERGY 367 Kcals/1540 KJ
FAT 5.36 g **SATURATED FAT** 0.60 g
CHOLESTEROL 0 **FIBRE** 6.76 g

Banana and Cardamom Bread

The combination of banana and cardamom is delicious in this soft-textured moist loaf. It is perfect for tea time, served with low fat spread and jam.

Serves 6

INGREDIENTS
150 ml/¼ pint/²⁄₃ cup warm water
5 ml/1 tsp dried yeast
pinch of sugar
10 cardamom pods
400 g/14 oz/3½ cups strong
   white flour
5 ml/1 tsp salt
30 ml/2 tbsp malt extract
2 ripe bananas, mashed
5 ml/1 tsp sesame seeds

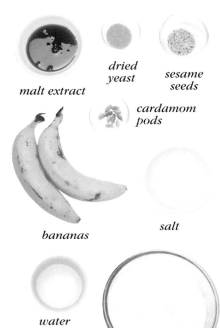

malt extract

dried yeast

sesame seeds

cardamom pods

bananas

salt

water

strong white flour

NUTRITIONAL NOTES

PER PORTION:

ENERGY 299 Kcals/1254 KJ
FAT 1.55 g **SATURATED FAT** 0.23 g
CHOLESTEROL 0 **FIBRE** 2.65 g

COOK'S TIP
Make sure the bananas are really ripe, so that they impart maximum flavour to the bread.

If you prefer, place the dough in one piece in a 450 g/1 lb loaf tin and bake for an extra 5 minutes.

1 Put the water in a small bowl. Sprinkle the yeast on top, add the sugar and mix well. Leave for 10 minutes.

2 Split the cardamom pods. Remove the seeds and chop them finely.

3 Sift the flour and salt into a mixing bowl and make a well in the centre. Add the yeast mixture with the malt extract, chopped cardamom seeds and bananas.

4 Gradually incorporate the flour and mix to a soft dough, adding a little extra water if necessary. Turn the dough on to a floured surface and knead for about 5 minutes until smooth and elastic. Return to the clean bowl, cover with a damp dish towel and leave to rise for about 2 hours until doubled in bulk.

5 Grease a baking sheet. Turn the dough on to a floured surface, knead briefly, then shape into a plait. Place the plait on the baking sheet and cover loosely with a plastic bag (ballooning it to trap the air). Leave until well risen. Preheat the oven to 220°C/425°F/Gas 7.

6 Brush the plait lightly with water and sprinkle with the sesame seeds. Bake for 10 minutes, then lower the oven temperature to 200°C/400°F/Gas 6. Cook for 15 minutes more, or until the loaf sounds hollow when it is tapped underneath. Cool on a wire rack.

Swedish Sultana Bread

A lightly sweetened bread that is delicious served warm. It is also excellent toasted and topped with low fat spread.

NUTRITIONAL NOTES
PER PORTION:

ENERGY 273 Kcals/1145 KJ
FAT 4.86 g **SATURATED FAT** 0.57 g
CHOLESTEROL 0.39 mg **FIBRE** 3.83 g

Serves 8–10

INGREDIENTS
150 ml/¹/₄ pint/²/₃ cup warm water
5 ml/1 tsp dried yeast
15 ml/1 tbsp clear honey
225 g/8 oz/2 cups wholemeal flour
225 g/8 oz/2 cups strong white flour
5 ml/1 tsp salt
115 g/4 oz/²/₃ cup sultanas
50 g/2 oz/¹/₂ cup walnuts, chopped
175 ml/6 fl oz/³/₄ cup warm skimmed
  milk, plus extra for glazing

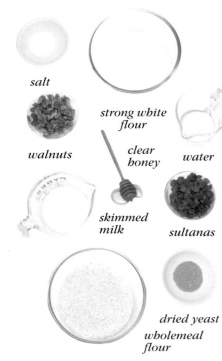

salt

strong white flour

walnuts

clear honey

water

skimmed milk

sultanas

dried yeast

wholemeal flour

VARIATION

To make Apple and Hazelnut Bread, replace the sultanas with 2 chopped eating apples and use chopped toasted hazelnuts instead of the walnuts. Add 5 ml/1 tsp ground cinnamon with the flour.

1 Put the water in a small bowl. Sprinkle the yeast on top. Add a few drops of the honey to help activate the yeast, mix well and leave for 10 minutes.

2 Put the flours in a bowl with the salt and sultanas. Set aside 15 ml/1 tbsp of the walnuts and add the rest to the bowl. Mix together lightly and make a well in the centre.

3 Add the yeast mixture to the flour mixture with the milk and remaining honey. Gradually incorporate the flour, mixing to a soft dough; add a little extra water if you need to.

4 Turn the dough on to a floured surface and knead for 5 minutes until smooth and elastic. Return to the clean bowl, cover with a damp dish towel and leave in a warm place to rise for about 2 hours until doubled in bulk. Grease a baking sheet.

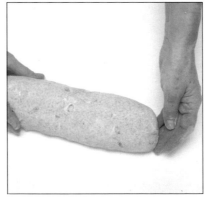

5 Turn the dough on to a floured surface and knead for 2 minutes, then shape into a 28 cm/11 in long sausage shape. Place the loaf on the prepared baking sheet. Make some diagonal cuts down the whole length of the loaf.

6 Brush the loaf with milk, sprinkle with the reserved walnuts and leave to rise for about 40 minutes. Preheat the oven to 220°C/425°F/Gas 7. Bake the loaf for 10 minutes. Lower the oven temperature to 200°C/400°F/Gas 6 and bake for about 20 minutes more, or until the loaf sounds hollow when it is tapped underneath.

Rye Bread

Rye bread is popular in Northern Europe and makes an excellent base for open sandwiches – add a low fat topping of your choice.

Makes 2 loaves, each serving 6

INGREDIENTS
475 ml/16 fl oz/2 cups warm water
10 ml/2 tsp dried yeast
pinch of sugar
350 g/12 oz/3 cups wholemeal flour
225 g/8 oz/2 cups rye flour
115 g/4 oz/1 cup strong white flour
7.5 ml/1½ tsp salt
30 ml/2 tbsp caraway seeds
30 ml/2 tbsp molasses
30 ml/2 tbsp sunflower oil

molasses
dried yeast
strong white flour

rye flour
wholemeal flour

salt
caraway seeds

sunflower oil
water

1 Put half the water in a jug. Sprinkle the yeast on top. Add the sugar, mix well and leave for 10 minutes.

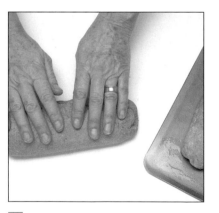

2 Put the flours and salt in a bowl. Set aside 5 ml/1 tsp of the caraway seeds and add the rest to the bowl.

3 Make a well in the flour mixture, then add the yeast mixture with the molasses, oil and the remaining water. Gradually incorporate the flour and mix to a soft dough, adding a little extra water if necessary.

4 Turn the dough on to a floured surface and knead for 5 minutes until smooth and elastic. Return to the clean bowl, cover with a damp dish towel and leave in a warm place to rise for about 2 hours until doubled in bulk. Grease a baking sheet.

5 Turn the dough on to a floured surface and knead for 2 minutes, then divide the dough in half, shape into two 23 cm/9 in long oval loaves. Flatten the loaves slightly and place them on the baking sheet.

6 Brush the loaves with water and sprinkle with the remaining caraway seeds. Cover and leave in a warm place for about 40 minutes until well risen. Preheat the oven to 200°C/400°F/Gas 6. Bake the loaves for 30 minutes, or until they sound hollow when they are tapped underneath. Cool on a wire rack. Serve the bread plain, or slice and add a low fat topping.

NUTRITIONAL NOTES
Per portion:

ENERGY 224 Kcals/941 KJ
FAT 3.43 g **SATURATED FAT** 0.33 g
CHOLESTEROL 0 **FIBRE** 6.04 g

VARIATION
Shape the dough into two loaves and bake in two greased 450 g/1 lb loaf tins, if you prefer.

Olive and Oregano Bread

This is an excellent accompaniment to all salads and is particularly good served warm.

Serves 8–10

NUTRITIONAL NOTES

PER PORTION:

ENERGY 202 Kcals/847 KJ
FAT 3.28 g **SATURATED FAT** 0.46 g
CHOLESTEROL 0 **FIBRE** 22.13 g

INGREDIENTS

300 ml/10 fl oz/1¼ cups warm water
5 ml/1 tsp dried yeast
pinch of sugar
15 ml/1 tbsp olive oil
1 onion, chopped
450 g/1 lb/4 cups strong white flour
5 ml/1 tsp salt
1.5 ml/¼ tsp freshly ground
  black pepper
50 g/2 oz/⅓ cup stoned black olives,
  roughly chopped
15 ml/1 tbsp black olive paste
15 ml/1 tbsp chopped fresh oregano
15 ml/1 tbsp chopped fresh parsley

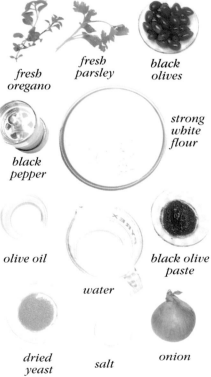

fresh oregano *fresh parsley* *black olives*

black pepper *strong white flour*

olive oil *black olive paste*

water

dried yeast *salt* *onion*

1 Put half the warm water in a jug. Sprinkle the yeast on top. Add the sugar, mix well and leave for 10 minutes.

2 Heat the olive oil in a frying pan and fry the onion until golden brown.

3 Sift the flour into a mixing bowl with the salt and pepper. Make a well in the centre. Add the yeast mixture, the fried onion (with the oil), the olives, olive paste, herbs and remaining water. Gradually incorporate the flour and mix to a soft dough, adding a little extra water if necessary.

4 Turn the dough on to a floured surface and knead for 5 minutes until smooth and elastic. Place in a mixing bowl, cover with a damp dish towel and leave in a warm place to rise for about 2 hours until doubled in bulk. Lightly grease a baking sheet.

5 Turn the dough on to a floured surface and knead again for a few minutes. Shape into a 20 cm/8 in round and place on the prepared baking sheet. Using a sharp knife, make criss-cross cuts over the top, cover and leave in a warm place for 30 minutes until well risen. Preheat the oven to 220°C/425°F/Gas 7.

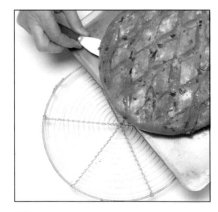

6 Dust the loaf with a little flour. Bake for 10 minutes then lower the oven temperature to 200°C/400°F/Gas 6. Bake for 20 minutes more, or until the loaf sounds hollow when it is tapped underneath. Transfer to a wire rack to cool slightly before serving.

Cheese and Onion Herb Sticks

An extremely tasty bread which is very good with soup or salads. Use an extra-strong cheese to give plenty of flavour without piling on the fat.

Makes 2 sticks, each serving 4–6

INGREDIENTS

300 ml/½ pint/1¼ cups warm water
5 ml/1 tsp dried yeast
pinch of sugar
15 ml/1 tbsp sunflower oil
1 red onion, chopped
450 g/1 lb/4 cups strong white flour
5 ml/1 tsp salt
5 ml/1 tsp dry mustard powder
45 ml/3 tbsp chopped fresh herbs,
  such as thyme, parsley, marjoram
  or sage
75 g/3 oz/¾ cup grated reduced-fat
  Cheddar cheese

fresh herbs

sunflower oil

reduced-fat Cheddar cheese

salt

mustard powder

strong white flour

red onion

water

dried yeast

1 Put the water in a jug. Sprinkle the yeast on top. Add the sugar, mix well and leave for 10 minutes.

2 Heat the oil in a frying pan and fry the onion until well coloured.

3 Sift the flour, salt and mustard into a mixing bowl. Add the herbs. Set aside 30 ml/2 tbsp of the cheese. Stir the rest into the flour mixture and make a well in the centre. Add the yeast mixture with the fried onions and oil, then gradually incorporate the flour and mix to a soft dough, adding extra water if necessary.

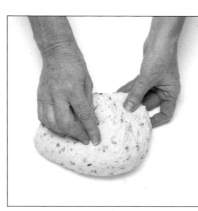

4 Turn the dough on to a floured surface and knead for 5 minutes until smooth and elastic. Return to the clean bowl, cover with a damp dish towel and leave in a warm place to rise for about 2 hours until doubled in bulk. Lightly grease two baking sheets.

5 Turn the dough on to a floured surface, knead briefly, then divide the mixture in half and roll each piece into a 30 cm/12 in long stick. Place each stick on a baking sheet and make diagonal cuts along the top.

NUTRITIONAL NOTES
PER PORTION:

ENERGY 210 Kcals/882 KJ
FAT 3.16 g **SATURATED FAT** 0.25 g
CHOLESTEROL 3.22 mg **FIBRE** 1.79 g

6 Sprinkle the sticks with the reserved cheese. Cover and leave for 30 minutes until well risen. Preheat the oven to 220°C/425°F/Gas 7. Bake the sticks for 25 minutes or until they sound hollow when they are tapped underneath. Cool on a wire rack.

VARIATION

To make Onion and Coriander Sticks, omit the cheese, herbs and mustard. Add 15 ml/1 tbsp ground coriander and 45 ml/3 tbsp chopped fresh coriander instead.

Sun-dried Tomato Plait

This is a marvellous Mediterranean-flavoured bread to serve at a summer buffet or barbecue.

Serves 8–10

NUTRITIONAL NOTES

PER PORTION:

ENERGY 294 Kcals/1233 KJ
FAT 12.12 g **SATURATED FAT** 2.13 g
CHOLESTEROL 3.40 mg **FIBRE** 3.39 g

COOK'S TIP
If you are unable to locate red pesto, use 30 ml/2 tbsp chopped fresh basil mixed with 15 ml/1 tbsp sun-dried tomato paste.

INGREDIENTS
300 ml/¹/₂ pint/1¹/₄ cups warm water
5 ml/1 tsp dried yeast
pinch of sugar
225 g/8 oz/2 cups wholemeal flour
225 g/8 oz/2 cups strong white flour
5 ml/1 tsp salt
1.5 ml/¹/₄ tsp freshly ground
    black pepper
115 g/4 oz/²/₃ cup drained sun-dried
    tomatoes in oil, chopped, plus
    15 ml/1 tbsp oil from the jar
25 g/1 oz/¹/₄ cup freshly grated
    Parmesan cheese
30 ml/2 tbsp red pesto
5 ml/1 tsp coarse sea salt

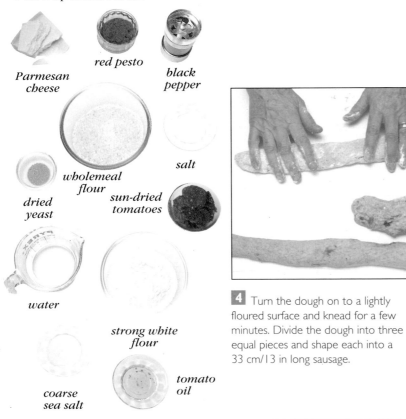

Parmesan cheese *red pesto* *black pepper*

dried yeast *wholemeal flour* *sun-dried tomatoes* *salt*

water

coarse sea salt *strong white flour* *tomato oil*

1 Put half the warm water in a jug. Sprinkle the yeast on top. Add the sugar, mix well and leave for 10 minutes.

2 Put the wholemeal flour in a mixing bowl. Sift in the white flour, salt and pepper. Make a well in the centre and add the yeast mixture, oil, sun-dried tomatoes, Parmesan, pesto and the remaining water. Gradually incorporate the flour and mix to a soft dough, adding a little extra water if necessary.

3 Turn the dough on to a floured surface and knead for 5 minutes until smooth and elastic. Return to the clean bowl, cover with a damp dish towel and leave in a warm place to rise for about 2 hours until doubled in bulk. Lightly grease a baking sheet.

4 Turn the dough on to a lightly floured surface and knead for a few minutes. Divide the dough into three equal pieces and shape each into a 33 cm/13 in long sausage.

5 Dampen the ends of the three "sausages". Press them together at one end, plait them loosely, then press them together at the other end. Place on the baking sheet, cover and leave in a warm place for 30 minutes until well risen. Preheat the oven to 220°C/425°F/Gas 7.

6 Sprinkle the plait with the coarse sea salt. Bake for 10 minutes, then lower the temperature to 200°C/400°F/Gas 6 and bake for a further 15–20 minutes, or until the loaf sounds hollow when tapped underneath. Cool on a wire rack.

Focaccia

This flat Italian bread is best served warm. It makes a delicious snack with low fat cheese and chunks of fresh tomato.

Serves 8

INGREDIENTS

300 ml/¹/₂ pint/1¹/₄ cups warm water
5 ml/1 tsp dried yeast
pinch of sugar
450 g/1 lb/4 cups strong white flour
5 ml/1 tsp salt
1.5 ml/¹/₄ tsp freshly ground
   black pepper
15 ml/1 tbsp pesto
115 g/4 oz/²/₃ cup stoned black
   olives, chopped
25 g/1 oz/3 tbsp drained sun-dried
   tomatoes in oil, chopped, plus
   15 ml/1 tbsp oil from the jar
5 ml/1 tsp coarse sea salt
5 ml/1 tsp roughly chopped
   fresh rosemary

1 Put the water in a bowl. Sprinkle the yeast on top. Add the sugar, mix well and leave for 10 minutes. Lightly grease a 33 × 23 cm/13 × 9 in Swiss roll tin.

2 Sift the flour, salt and pepper into a bowl and make a well in the centre.

3 Add the yeast mixture with the pesto, olives and sun-dried tomatoes (reserve the oil). Mix to a soft dough, adding a little extra water if necessary.

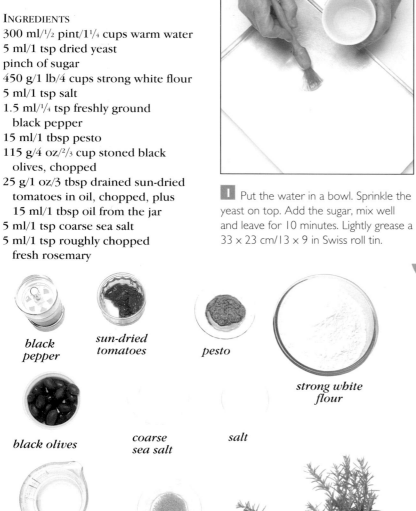

black pepper

sun-dried tomatoes

pesto

strong white flour

black olives

coarse sea salt

salt

water

dried yeast

fresh rosemary

tomato oil

4 Turn the dough on to a floured surface and knead for 5 minutes until smooth and elastic. Return to the clean bowl, cover with a damp dish towel and leave in a warm place to rise for about 2 hours until doubled in bulk.

5 Turn the dough on to a floured surface, knead briefly, then roll out to a 33 × 23 cm/13 × 9 in rectangle. Lift the dough over the rolling pin and place in the prepared tin. Preheat the oven to 220°C/425°F/Gas 7.

NUTRITIONAL NOTES

PER PORTION:

ENERGY 247 Kcals/1038 KJ
FAT 6.42 g **SATURATED FAT** 0.93 g
CHOLESTEROL 0.35 mg **FIBRE** 2.18 g

6 Using your fingertips, make small indentations all over the dough. Brush with the reserved oil from the sun-dried tomatoes, then sprinkle with the salt and rosemary. Leave to rise for 20 minutes, then bake for 20–25 minutes, or until golden. Transfer to a wire rack, but serve while still warm.

VARIATION

To make Oregano and Onion Focaccia, omit the pesto, olives and sun-dried tomatoes. Add 15 ml/ 1 tbsp chopped fresh oregano or 5 ml/1 tsp dried oregano to the flour. Slice 1 onion very thinly into rounds and scatter over the rolled out dough. Drizzle with olive oil and sprinkle with sea salt before baking.

Spinach and Bacon Bread

This bread is so tasty that it is a good idea to make double the quantity and freeze one of the loaves. Use smoked lean back bacon for the best possible flavour with the minimum of fat.

NUTRITIONAL NOTES

PER PORTION:

ENERGY 172 Kcals/723 KJ
FAT 2.17 g **SATURATED FAT** 0.36 g
CHOLESTEROL 1.97 mg **FIBRE** 1.68 g

Makes 2 loaves, each serving 8

INGREDIENTS
450 ml/³/₄ pint/2 cups warm water
10 ml/2 tsp dried yeast
pinch of sugar
15 ml/1 tbsp olive oil
1 onion, chopped
115 g/4 oz rindless smoked bacon
   rashers, chopped
225 g/8 oz chopped spinach, thawed
   if frozen
675 g/1¹/₂ lb/6 cups strong
   plain flour
7.5 ml/1¹/₂ tsp salt
2.5 ml/¹/₂ tsp grated nutmeg
25 g/1 oz/¹/₄ cup grated reduced-fat
   Cheddar cheese

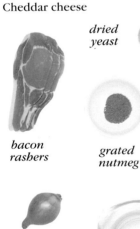

bacon
rashers

*dried
yeast*

*grated
nutmeg*

onion

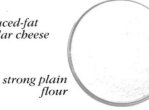

spinach

water

*reduced-fat
Cheddar cheese*

olive oil

salt

*strong plain
flour*

1 Put the water in a small bowl. Sprinkle the yeast on top and add the sugar. Mix well and leave for 10 minutes. Lightly grease two 23 cm/9 in cake tins.

2 Heat the oil in a frying pan and fry the onion and bacon for 10 minutes until golden brown. Meanwhile, if using frozen spinach, drain it thoroughly.

3 Sift the flour, salt and nutmeg into a mixing bowl and make a well in the centre. Add the yeast mixture. Tip in the fried bacon and onion (with the oil), then add the spinach. Gradually incorporate the flour mixture and mix to a soft dough.

4 Turn the dough on to a floured surface and knead for 5 minutes until smooth and elastic. Return to the clean bowl, cover with a damp dish towel and leave in a warm place to rise for about 2 hours until doubled in bulk.

COOK'S TIP

If using frozen spinach, be sure to squeeze out any excess liquid or the resulting dough will be too sticky.

5 Turn the dough on to a floured surface, knead briefly then divide it in half. Shape each half into a ball, flatten slightly and place in a tin, pressing the dough so that it extends to the edges. Mark each loaf into eight wedges and sprinkle with the cheese. Cover loosely with a plastic bag and leave in a warm place until well risen. Preheat the oven to 200°C/400°F/Gas 6.

6 Bake the loaves for 25–30 minutes, or until they sound hollow when they are tapped underneath. Transfer to a wire rack to cool.

Malt Loaf

This is a rich and sticky loaf. If it lasts long enough to go stale, try toasting it for a delicious tea-time treat.

NUTRITIONAL NOTES

PER PORTION:

ENERGY 279 Kcals/1171 KJ
FAT 2.06 g **SATURATED FAT** 0.33 g
CHOLESTEROL 0.38 mg **FIBRE** 1.79 g

Serves 8

INGREDIENTS
150 ml/¼ pint/⅔ cup warm
   skimmed milk
5 ml/1 tsp dried yeast
pinch of caster sugar
350 g/12 oz/3 cups plain flour
1.5 ml/¼ tsp salt
30 ml/2 tbsp light muscovado sugar
175 g/6 oz/generous 1 cup sultanas
15 ml/1 tbsp sunflower oil
45 ml/3 tbsp malt extract

FOR THE GLAZE
30 ml/2 tbsp caster sugar
30 ml/2 tbsp water

sultanas

malt extract

salt

plain flour

skimmed milk

light muscovado sugar

dried yeast

sunflower oil

VARIATION

To make buns, divide the dough into 10 pieces, shape into rounds, leave to rise, then bake for about 15–20 minutes. Brush with the glaze while still hot.

1 Place the warm milk in a bowl. Sprinkle the yeast on top and add the sugar. Leave for 30 minutes until frothy. Sift the flour and salt into a mixing bowl, stir in the muscovado sugar and sultanas, and make a well in the centre.

2 Add the yeast mixture with the oil and malt extract. Gradually incorporate the flour and mix to a soft dough, adding a little extra milk if necessary.

3 Turn on to a floured surface and knead for about 5 minutes until smooth and elastic. Grease a 450 g/1 lb loaf tin.

4 Shape the dough and place it in the prepared tin. Cover with a damp dish towel and leave in a warm place for 1–2 hours until well risen. Preheat the oven to 190°C/375°F/Gas 5.

5 Bake the loaf for 30–35 minutes, or until it sounds hollow when it is tapped underneath.

6 Meanwhile, prepare the glaze by dissolving the sugar in the water in a small pan. Bring to the boil, stirring, then lower the heat and simmer for 1 minute. Place the loaf on a wire rack and brush with the glaze while still hot. Leave the loaf to cool before serving.

Cinnamon Apple Gâteau

Make this lovely cake for an autumn celebration.

Serves 8

NUTRITIONAL NOTES
PER PORTION:

ENERGY 244 Kcals/1023 KJ
FAT 4.05 g SATURATED FAT 1.71 g
CHOLESTEROL 77.95 mg FIBRE 1.50 g

INGREDIENTS
3 eggs
115 g/4 oz/¹/₂ cup caster sugar
75 g/3 oz/³/₄ cup plain flour
5 ml/1 tsp ground cinnamon

FOR THE FILLING AND TOPPING
4 large eating apples
60 ml/4 tbsp clear honey
15 ml/1 tbsp water
75 g/3 oz/¹/₂ cup sultanas
2.5 ml/¹/₂ tsp ground cinnamon
350 g/12 oz/1¹/₂ cups low fat
  soft cheese
60 ml/4 tbsp reduced-fat
  fromage frais
10 ml/2 tsp lemon juice
45 ml/3 tbsp Apricot Glaze
mint sprigs, to decorate

eggs

eating apples

plain flour

reduced-fat fromage frais

lemon

caster sugar

low fat soft cheese

sultanas

Apricot Glaze

clear honey

ground cinnamon

1 Preheat the oven to 190°C/375°F/ Gas 5. Grease and line a 23 cm/9 in sandwich cake tin. Place the eggs and caster sugar in a bowl and beat with a hand-held electric whisk until thick and mousse-like (when the whisk is lifted, a trail should remain on the surface of the mixture for at least 15 seconds).

2 Sift the flour and cinnamon over the egg mixture and carefully fold in with a large spoon. Pour into the prepared tin and bake for 25–30 minutes or until the cake springs back when lightly pressed. Slide a palette knife between the cake and the tin to loosen the edge, then turn the cake on to a wire rack to cool.

3 To make the filling, peel, core and slice three of the apples and put them in a saucepan. Add 30 ml/2 tbsp of the honey and the water. Cover and cook over a gentle heat for about 10 minutes until the apples have softened. Add the sultanas and cinnamon, stir well, replace the lid and leave to cool.

4 Put the soft cheese in a bowl with the remaining honey, the fromage frais and half the lemon juice. Beat until the mixture is smooth.

5 Halve the cake horizontally, place the bottom half on a board and drizzle over any liquid from the apples. Spread with two-thirds of the cheese mixture, then top with the apple filling. Fit the top of the cake in place.

6 Swirl the remaining cheese mixture over the top of the sponge. Core and slice the remaining apple, sprinkle with lemon juice and use to decorate the edge of the cake. Brush the apple with Apricot Glaze and place mint sprigs on top, to decorate.

Chestnut and Orange Roulade

This moist cake is ideal to serve as a dessert.

NUTRITIONAL NOTES

PER PORTION:

ENERGY 185 Kcals/775 KJ
FAT 4.01 g **SATURATED FAT** 1.47 g
CHOLESTEROL 76.25 mg **FIBRE** 1.40 g

Serves 8

INGREDIENTS
3 eggs, separated
115 g/4 oz/$\frac{1}{2}$ cup caster sugar
$\frac{1}{2}$ x 439 g/15$\frac{1}{2}$ oz can unsweetened
  chestnut purée
grated rind and juice of 1 orange
icing sugar, for dusting

FOR THE FILLING
225 g/8 oz/1 cup low fat soft cheese
15 ml/1 tbsp clear honey
1 orange

eggs

*unsweetened
chestnut purée*

*clear
honey*

caster sugar

oranges

*low fat
soft cheese*

COOK'S TIP
Do not whisk the egg whites too stiffly, or it will be difficult to fold them into the mixture and they will form lumps in the roulade.

1 Preheat the oven to 180°C/350°F/ Gas 4. Grease a 30 x 20 cm/12 x 8 in Swiss roll tin and line with non-stick baking paper. Whisk the egg yolks and sugar in a bowl until thick and creamy.

4 Spoon the roulade mixture into the prepared tin and bake for 30 minutes until firm. Cool for 5 minutes, then cover with a clean damp dish towel and leave until completely cold.

2 Put the chestnut purée in a separate bowl. Whisk in the orange rind and juice, then whisk the flavoured chestnut purée into the egg mixture.

5 Meanwhile, make the filling. Put the soft cheese in a bowl with the honey. Finely grate the orange rind and add to the bowl. Peel away all the pith from the orange, cut the fruit into segments, chop roughly and set aside. Add any juice to the cheese mixture, then beat until it is smooth. Mix in the chopped orange.

3 Whisk the egg whites in a grease-free bowl until fairly stiff. Using a metal spoon, stir a generous spoonful of the whites into the chestnut mixture to lighten it, then fold in the rest.

6 Sprinkle a sheet of greaseproof paper thickly with icing sugar. Carefully turn the roulade out on to the paper, then peel off the lining paper. Spread the filling over the roulade and roll up like a Swiss roll. Transfer to a plate and dust with some more icing sugar.

Nectarine Amaretto Cake

Try this delicious cake with low fat fromage frais for dessert, or serve it solo for afternoon tea. The syrup makes it moist but not soggy.

Serves 8

NUTRITIONAL NOTES

PER PORTION:

ENERGY 264 Kcals/1108 KJ
FAT 5.70 g **SATURATED FAT** 0.85 g
CHOLESTEROL 72.19 mg **FIBRE** 1.08 g

INGREDIENTS

3 eggs, separated
175 g/6 oz/³/₄ cup caster sugar
grated rind and juice of 1 lemon
50 g/2 oz/¹/₃ cup semolina
40 g/1¹/₂ oz/¹/₃ cup ground almonds
25 g/1 oz/¹/₄ cup plain flour
2 nectarines or peaches, halved
   and stoned
60 ml/4 tbsp Apricot Glaze

FOR THE SYRUP

75 g/3 oz/6 tbsp caster sugar
90 ml/6 tbsp water
30 ml/2 tbsp Amaretto liqueur

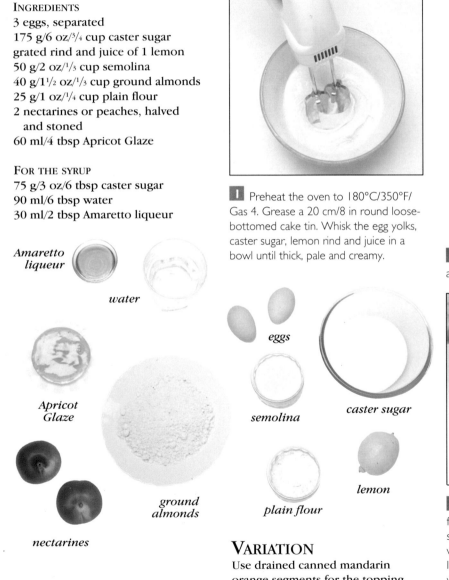

Amaretto liqueur

water

eggs

Apricot Glaze

semolina

caster sugar

ground almonds

plain flour

lemon

nectarines

1 Preheat the oven to 180°C/350°F/ Gas 4. Grease a 20 cm/8 in round loose-bottomed cake tin. Whisk the egg yolks, caster sugar, lemon rind and juice in a bowl until thick, pale and creamy.

2 Fold in the semolina, almonds and flour until smooth.

3 Whisk the egg whites in a grease-free bowl until fairly stiff. Using a metal spoon, stir a generous spoonful of the whites into the semolina mixture to lighten it, then fold in the remaining egg whites. Spoon the mixture into the prepared cake tin.

4 Bake for 30–35 minutes until the centre of the cake springs back when lightly pressed. Remove the cake from the oven and carefully loosen around the edge with a palette knife. Prick the top of the cake with a skewer and leave to cool slightly in the tin.

VARIATION

Use drained canned mandarin orange segments for the topping, if preferred, and use an orange-flavoured liqueur instead of the Amaretto.

5 Meanwhile, make the syrup. Heat the sugar and water in a small pan, stirring until dissolved, then boil without stirring for 2 minutes. Add the Amaretto liqueur and drizzle slowly over the cake.

6 Remove the cake from the tin and transfer it to a serving plate. Slice the nectarines or peaches, arrange them over the top and brush with the warm Apricot Glaze.

Strawberry Gâteau

It is hard to believe that this delicious gâteau is low in fat, but it is true, so enjoy!

Serves 6

NUTRITIONAL NOTES

PER PORTION:

ENERGY 213 Kcals/893 KJ
FAT 6.08 g **SATURATED FAT** 1.84 g
CHOLESTEROL 70.22 mg **FIBRE** 1.02 g

VARIATION

Use other soft fruits in season, such as currants, raspberries, blackberries or blueberries, or try a mixture of different berries.

INGREDIENTS
2 eggs
75 g/3 oz/6 tbsp caster sugar
grated rind of ½ orange
50 g/2 oz/½ cup plain flour
strawberry leaves, to decorate
icing sugar, for dusting

FOR THE FILLING
275 g/10 oz/1¼ cups low fat
  soft cheese
grated rind of ½ orange
30 ml/2 tbsp caster sugar
60 ml/4 tbsp low fat
  fromage frais
225 g/8 oz strawberries, halved
25 g/1 oz/¼ cup chopped
  almonds, toasted

low fat fromage frais

eggs

strawberries

low fat soft cheese

caster sugar

almonds

orange

plain flour

1 Preheat the oven to 190°C/375°F/Gas 5. Grease a 30 x 20 cm/12 x 8 in Swiss roll tin and line with non-stick baking paper.

2 In a bowl, whisk the eggs, sugar and orange rind together with a hand-held electric whisk until thick and mousse-like (when the whisk is lifted, a trail should remain on the surface of the mixture for at least 15 seconds).

3 Fold in the flour with a metal spoon, being careful not to knock out any air. Turn into the prepared tin. Bake for 15–20 minutes, or until the cake springs back when lightly pressed. Turn the cake on to a wire rack, remove the lining paper and leave to cool.

4 Meanwhile make the filling. In a bowl, mix the soft cheese with the orange rind, sugar and fromage frais until smooth. Divide between two bowls. Chop half the strawberry halves and add to one bowl of filling.

5 Cut the sponge widthways into three equal pieces and sandwich them together with the strawberry filling. Spread two-thirds of the plain filling over the sides of the cake and press on the toasted almonds.

6 Spread the rest of the filling over the top of the cake and decorate with the strawberry halves, and strawberry leaves if liked. Dust with icing sugar and transfer to a serving plate.

Tia Maria Gâteau

A feather-light coffee sponge with a creamy liqueur-flavoured filling.

NUTRITIONAL NOTES

PER PORTION:

ENERGY 226 Kcals/951 KJ
FAT 3.14 g **SATURATED FAT** 1.17 g
CHOLESTEROL 75.03 mg **FIBRE** 0.64 g

Serves 8

INGREDIENTS
75 g/3 oz/³/₄ cup plain flour
30 ml/2 tbsp instant coffee powder
3 eggs
115 g/4 oz/¹/₂ cup caster sugar
coffee beans, to decorate (optional)

FOR THE FILLING
175 g/6 oz/³/₄ cup low fat soft cheese
15 ml/1 tbsp clear honey
15 ml/1 tbsp Tia Maria
50 g/2 oz/¹/₄ cup stem ginger,
    roughly chopped

FOR THE ICING
225 g/8 oz/1³/₄ cups icing
    sugar, sifted
10 ml/2 tsp coffee essence
15 ml/1 tbsp water
5 ml/1 tsp fat-reduced cocoa powder

1 Preheat the oven to 190°C/375°F/ Gas 5. Grease and line a 20 cm/8 in deep round cake tin. Sift the flour and coffee powder together on to a sheet of greaseproof paper.

2 Whisk the eggs and sugar in a bowl with a hand-held electric whisk until thick and mousse-like (when the whisk is lifted, a trail should remain on the surface of the mixture for at least 15 seconds).

3 Gently fold in the flour mixture with a metal spoon, being careful not to knock out any air. Turn the mixture into the prepared tin. Bake the sponge for 30–35 minutes or until it springs back when lightly pressed. Turn on to a wire rack and leave to cool completely.

clear honey
eggs
coffee beans
coffee essence
low fat soft cheese
coffee powder
stem ginger
plain flour
icing sugar
caster sugar
fat-reduced cocoa powder
Tia Maria

4 Make the filling. Mix the soft cheese with the honey in a bowl. Beat until smooth, then stir in the Tia Maria and chopped stem ginger.

5 Split the cake in half horizontally and sandwich the two halves together with the Tia Maria filling.

6 Make the icing. In a bowl, mix the icing sugar and coffee essence with enough of the water to make an icing which will coat the back of a wooden spoon. Pour three-quarters of the icing over the cake, spreading it evenly to the edges. Stir the cocoa into the remaining icing until smooth. Spoon into a piping bag fitted with a writing nozzle and pipe the mocha icing over the coffee icing. Decorate with coffee beans, if liked.

VARIATION
To make a Mocha Gâteau, replace the coffee powder with 30 ml/2 tbsp fat-reduced cocoa powder, sifting it with the flour. Omit the chopped ginger in the filling.

Raspberry Vacherin

Meringue rounds filled with orange-flavoured fromage frais and fresh raspberries make a perfect dinner party dessert.

NUTRITIONAL NOTES
PER PORTION:

ENERGY 248 Kcals/1041 KJ
FAT 2.22 g **SATURATED FAT** 0.82 g
CHOLESTEROL 4.00 mg **FIBRE** 1.06 g

Serves 6

INGREDIENTS
3 egg whites
175 g/6 oz/³/₄ cup caster sugar
5 ml/1 tsp chopped almonds
icing sugar, for dusting
raspberry leaves, to decorate

FOR THE FILLING
175 g/6 oz/³/₄ cup low fat soft cheese
15–30 ml/1–2 tbsp clear honey
15 ml/1 tbsp Cointreau
120 ml/4 fl oz/¹/₂ cup low fat
   fromage frais
225 g/8 oz raspberries

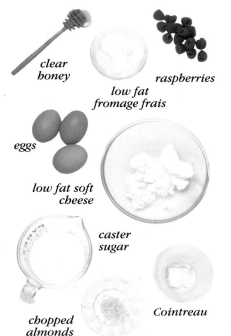

clear honey

raspberries

low fat fromage frais

eggs

low fat soft cheese

caster sugar

chopped almonds

Cointreau

COOK'S TIP
When making the meringue, whisk the egg whites until they are so stiff that you can turn the bowl upside-down without them falling out.

1 Preheat the oven to 140°C/275°F/ Gas 1. Draw a 20 cm/8 in circle on two pieces of non-stick baking paper. Turn the paper over so the marking is on the underside and use it to line two heavy baking sheets.

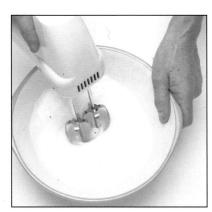

2 Whisk the egg whites in a grease-free bowl until very stiff, then gradually whisk in the caster sugar to make a stiff meringue mixture.

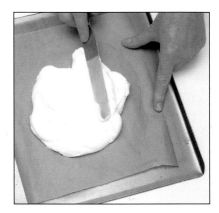

3 Spoon the mixture on to the circles on the prepared baking sheets, spreading the meringue evenly to the edges. Sprinkle one meringue round with the chopped almonds.

4 Bake for 1½–2 hours, then carefully lift the meringue rounds off the baking sheets, peel away the paper and cool on a wire rack.

5 To make the filling, cream the soft cheese with the honey and liqueur in a bowl. Fold in the fromage frais and raspberries, reserving three of the best for decoration.

6 Place the plain meringue round on a board, spread with the filling and top with the nut-covered round. Dust with icing sugar, transfer to a serving plate and decorate with the reserved raspberries, and a sprig of raspberry leaves, if liked.

Lemon Chiffon Cake

Lemon mousse provides a tangy filling for this light lemon sponge.

Serves 8

INGREDIENTS
2 eggs
75 g/3 oz/6 tbsp caster sugar
grated rind of 1 lemon
50 g/2 oz/¹/₂ cup sifted plain flour
Lemon Shreds, to decorate

FOR THE FILLING
2 eggs, separated
75 g/3 oz/6 tbsp caster sugar
grated rind and juice of 1 lemon
30 ml/2 tbsp water
15 ml/1 tbsp gelatine
125 ml/4 fl oz/¹/₂ cup low fat
   fromage frais

FOR THE ICING
115 g/4 oz/scant 1 cup icing
   sugar, sifted
15 ml/1 tbsp lemon juice

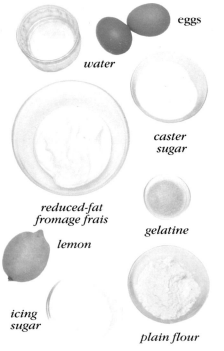

eggs

water

caster
sugar

reduced-fat
fromage frais

gelatine

lemon

icing
sugar

plain flour

1 Preheat the oven to 180°C/350°F/ Gas 4. Grease and line a 20 cm/8 in loose-bottomed cake tin. Whisk the eggs, sugar and lemon rind together with a hand-held electric whisk until thick and mousse-like. Gently fold in the flour, then turn the mixture into the prepared tin.

2 Bake for 20–25 minutes until the cake springs back when lightly pressed in the centre. Turn on to a wire rack to cool. Once cold, split the cake in half horizontally and return the lower half to the clean cake tin. Set aside.

3 Make the filling. Place the egg yolks, sugar, lemon rind and juice in a bowl. Beat with a hand-held electric whisk until thick, pale and creamy.

4 Pour the water into a small heat-proof bowl and sprinkle the gelatine on top. Leave until spongy, then place over simmering water and stir until dissolved. Cool slightly, then whisk into the yolk mixture. Fold in the fromage frais. When the mixture begins to set, quickly whisk the egg whites to soft peaks. Fold a spoonful into the mousse mixture to lighten it, then fold in the rest.

5 Pour the lemon mousse over the sponge in the cake tin, spreading it to the edges. Set the second layer of sponge on top and chill until set.

6 Slide a palette knife dipped in hot water between the tin and the cake to loosen it, then carefully transfer the cake to a serving plate. Make the icing by adding enough lemon juice to the icing sugar to make a mixture thick enough to coat the back of a wooden spoon. Pour over the cake and spread evenly to the edges. Decorate with the Lemon Shreds.

NUTRITIONAL NOTES
PER PORTION:

ENERGY 202 Kcals/849 KJ
FAT 2.81 g **SATURATED FAT** 0.79 g
CHOLESTEROL 96.41 mg **FIBRE** 0.20 g

COOK'S TIP
The mousse mixture should be just on the point of setting when the egg whites are added. This setting process can be speeded up by placing the bowl of mousse in a bowl of iced water.

INDEX

A

Almonds:
  apricot and almond fingers, 33
  mango and amaretti
    strudel, 40
  nectarine Amaretto cake, 86
Amaretti biscuits:
  filo and apricot purses, 26
  mango and amaretti strudel, 40
Amaretto liqueur:
  nectarine Amaretto cake, 86
Angel cake, 42
Apples:
  apple and hazelnut bread, 66
  cinnamon apple gâteau, 82
  date and apple muffins, 31
  spiced apple cake, 47
Apricots:
  apricot and almond fingers, 33
  apricot glaze, 21
  banana and apricot Chelsea
    buns, 28
  filo and apricot purses, 26
  filo scrunchies, 27
Austrian three-grain bread, 62

B

Bacon:
  spinach and bacon bread, 78
Baking tins, lining, 18
Bananas:
  banana and apricot Chelsea
    buns, 28
  banana and cardamom
    bread, 64
  banana and ginger teabread, 46
  banana and sultana
    teabread, 46
  banana gingerbread slices, 22
  chocolate banana cake, 38
Baps, granary, 54
Biscuits:
  curry crackers, 56
  oatcakes, 57
  oaty crisps, 35
Breads, 60–80
  apple and hazelnut bread, 66
  Austrian three-grain bread, 62
  banana and cardamom
    bread, 64
  caraway bread sticks, 49
  cheese and onion herb
    sticks, 72
  coriander and sesame sticks, 49
  focaccia, 76
  granary baps, 54
  malt loaf, 80

olive and oregano bread, 70
onion and coriander sticks, 73
oregano and onion focaccia, 77
Parma ham and Parmesan
  bread, 61
poppy seed rolls, 50
rye bread, 68
soda bread, 60
spinach and bacon bread, 78
sun-dried tomato plait, 74
Swedish sultana bread, 66
Buns:
  banana and apricot Chelsea
    buns, 28

C

Caraway bread sticks, 49
Cardamom:
  banana and cardamom
    bread, 64
Cheese:
  cheese and onion herb
    sticks, 72
  Parma ham and Parmesan
    bread, 61
Chelsea buns, banana and
  apricot, 28
Chestnut and orange
  roulade, 84
Chive and potato scones, 52
Chocolate:
  chocolate banana cake, 38
Cinnamon:
  cinnamon apple gâteau, 82
  pineapple and cinnamon drop
    scones, 59
Citrus fruits, 21
Coffee:
  coffee sponge drops, 34
  Tia Maria gâteau, 90
Coriander:
  coriander and sesame
    sticks, 49
  onion and coriander sticks, 73
Curry crackers, 56

D

Dates:
  date and apple muffins, 31
  spiced apple cake, 47

Drop scones, 58
  pineapple and cinnamon, 59

F

Filo pastry:
  filo and apricot purses, 26
  filo scrunchies, 27
Focaccia, 76
  oregano and onion focaccia, 77
Fruit cakes:
  fruit and nut cake, 37
  Irish whiskey cake, 36

G

Gâteaux:
  chestnut and orange
    roulade, 84
  cinnamon apple gâteau, 82
  lemon chiffon cake, 94
  mocha gâteau, 91
  nectarine Amaretto cake, 86
  raspberry vacherin, 92
  strawberry gâteau, 88
  Tia Maria gâteau, 90
Ginger:
  banana and ginger teabread, 46
  banana gingerbread slices, 22
Granary baps, 54

H

Ham:
  ham and tomato scones, 53
  Parma ham and Parmesan
    bread, 61
Hazelnuts:
  apple and hazelnut bread, 66

I

Icing a cake, 20
Icing bag, making, 20
Irish whiskey cake, 36

L

Large cakes:
  angel cake, 42
  chocolate banana cake, 38
  spiced apple cake, 47
  see also Fruit cakes; Gâteaux;
    Swiss rolls; Teabreads
Lemon:
  lemon chiffon cake, 94
  lemon shreds, 21
  lemon sponge fingers, 24

M

Malt loaf, 80
Mango and amaretti strudel, 40

Meringues:
  muscovado meringues, 32
  pineapple snowballs, 25
  raspberry vacherin, 92
  snowballs, 25
Mocha gâteau, 91
Muffins:
  date and apple, 31
  raspberry, 30
Muscovado meringues, 32

N

Nectarines:
  nectarine Amaretto cake, 86

O

Oats:
  oatcakes, 57
  oaty crisps, 35
Olive and oregano bread, 70
Onions:
  cheese and onion herb
    sticks, 72
  onion and coriander sticks, 73
  oregano and onion focaccia, 77
Orange:
  chestnut and orange
    roulade, 84
  spicy orange fingers, 24
Oregano:
  olive and oregano bread, 70
  oregano and onion focaccia, 77

P

Parma ham and Parmesan
  bread, 61
Pastries:
  filo and apricot purses, 26
  filo scrunchies, 27
Peaches:
  peach Swiss roll, 44
Pear and sultana teabread, 43
Pineapple:
  pineapple and cinnamon drop
    scones, 59
  pineapple snowballs, 25
Poppy seed rolls, 50

R

Raspberries:
  raspberry muffins, 30
  raspberry vacherin, 92
Rolls:
  poppy seed rolls, 50
  shaping rolls, 17
Roulade, chestnut and
  orange, 84

Rye bread, 68

S

Scones:
  chive and potato scones, 52
  drop scones, 58
  ham and tomato scones, 53
  pineapple and cinnamon drop
    scones, 59
Sesame seeds:
  coriander and sesame sticks, 49
Snowballs, 25
Soda bread, 60
Spiced apple cake, 47
Spinach and bacon bread, 78
Sponge drops, coffee, 34
Sponge fingers:
  hazelnut, 24
  lemon, 24
Strawberry gâteau, 88
Strudel, mango and amaretti, 40
Sultanas:
  pear and sultana teabread, 43
  Swedish sultana bread, 66
Sun-dried tomato plait, 74
Sun-dried tomato triangles, 48
Swedish sultana bread, 66
Swiss roll, peach, 44

T

Teabreads:
  banana and ginger, 46
  banana and sultana, 46
  pear and sultana, 43
Testing cakes, 19
Tia Maria gâteau, 90
Tomatoes:
  ham and tomato scones, 53
  sun-dried tomato plait, 74
  sun-dried tomato triangles, 48

W

Whiskey:
  Irish whiskey cake, 36
Wholemeal herb triangles, 48

Y

Yeast, 16, 51